THE CALEDONIAN PHALANX
SCOTS IN RUSSIA

St Pantaleimon's Bridge over the Fontanka in St Petersburg, built by Charles Baird (see p. 70).

THE CALEDONIAN PHALANX

SCOTS · IN · RUSSIA

NATIONAL LIBRARY OF SCOTLAND
EDINBURGH
1987

© National Library of Scotland 1987

All rights reserved. No part of this publication may be reproduced, stored in a retrieval system, or transmitted in any form or by any means, electronic, mechanical, photocopying, recording or otherwise, without the prior permission of the National Library of Scotland.

British Library Cataloguing in Publication Data
The Caledonian Phalanx: Scots in Russia.
   1. Soviet Union——Civilization——Scottish Influences
   I. Dukes, Paul, *1934-*
   947'. 0049163   DK32   ISBN 0-902220-88-8

Note: 'The Caledonian Phalanx' was a phrase used in 1805 by Zacchaeus Walker, then working in the Mint at St Petersburg to his uncle, the industrialist Matthew Boulton (see p. 74). Cited by Professor Eric Robinson in his article, 'The transference of British technology to Russia, 1760-1820: a preliminary enquiry', in *Great Britain and the World, 1750-1914: Essays in honour of W. O. Henderson,* ed. B. M. Ratcliffe, Manchester, 1975.

The National Library of Scotland acknowledges with gratitude the co-operation and assistance of the Scottish Branch of the Great Britain-USSR Association in the preparation of the Scotland and Russia exhibition, and the accompanying publication.

Cover illustration:
Monastery near Archangel sketched by J. F. Campbell of Islay.

ISBN 0 902220 88 8

CONTENTS

Introduction	7
Scottish Soldiers in Muscovy by Paul Dukes	9
Scoto-Russian Contacts in the Reign of Catherine the Great (1762-1796) by A. G. Cross	24
Through the Looking-Glass: Scottish Doctors in Russia (1704-1854) by John H. Appleby	47
From the Banks of the Neva to the Shores of Lake Baikal: Some Enterprising Scots in Russia by John R. Bowles	65
Caledonia and Rus': some Literary Cross-References by Ian McGowan	81
The Carricks of St Petersburg by Felicity Ashbee	91

ACKNOWLEDGEMENTS

The Trustees of the National Library of Scotland wish to express their gratitude to owners, private and institutional, who have provided photographs in the publication: Miss F. Ashbee; Professor R. C. Bawden; Dr P. Dukes; Mr J. G. James; Mr D. Shvidkovskii; Dr J. B. Wilson; Glasgow University Archives; The Library of the Wellcome Institute; and the National Trust for Scotland.

INTRODUCTION

THE exhibition on the connexions between Scotland and Russia, which this publication is designed to accompany, was inspired by a suggestion from the Scottish Branch of the Great Britain-USSR Association, and seems particularly appropriate for a year when the Edinburgh International Festival has a Russian theme. The exhibition also fits into a series organized by the National Library on the links between Scotland and countries abroad, where Scots have made a substantial contribution to their development.

Like the exhibition, this publication is not intended to provide a comprehensive account of the contacts and relations between Scotland and Russia throughout their respective histories. However, the essays illustrate many of the more important contributions made by Scots to the varied history of Russia, and the final essay gives a vivid account of the detail of one Scottish family's connexion with that land.

Thanks are due to all the contributors to this volume who have generously agreed to be associated with the Library in this publication to mark the occasion of the Scotland and Russia exhibition.

E. F. D. Roberts
Librarian
June 1987

SCOTTISH SOLDIERS IN MUSCOVY
PAUL DUKES

PERHAPS the earliest literary reference to Britons in Russia was made by Chaucer in the Prologue to his Canterbury Tales, where he wrote of the Knight who had:

... often sat at table in the chair of honour, above all nations, when in Prussia. In Lithuania he had ridden, and Russia ...

By the time of the composition of Chaucer's masterpiece in the late 14th century, several Scottish as well as English knights had in fact participated in the Baltic crusade of the Teutonic Knights, thus beginning a real-life epic that stretched up to more recent times.

The attempt of the Teutonic Knights to spread Roman Catholicism from Prussia to Lithuania and beyond aroused the chivalric instincts of a considerable number of fighting men from varied origins. Among the Scots who answered the call were the brothers Norman and Walter Leslie in 1356, David de Berclay in 1362 and Adam de Hepburn in 1378. Already, the rivalry between English and Scots was making itself felt far away from Borders battlefields. A Prussian chronicler described a fracas in Königsberg in 1391:

Meanwhile there was dissension on the part of the English and Scots. Indeed, the Scot Sir William de Duclos [that is, Sir William Douglas of Nithsdale] *was killed near the high point of the bridge; he defended himself manfully when he fell with one leg into a hole, and was killed there together with one of his household.*

At about this time, there were several other Scots both identified and anonymous in the ranks of the Teutonic Knights. For example, another Douglas, Sir James, possibly of the Dalkeith branch of the family, acknowledged in Danzig a debt to Sir Robert Stewart of Durisdeer, and Sir John de Abernethy went over to Prussia with two servants and harness. Among those involved in the battle of Tannenberg in 1410, which brought the Baltic crusade to an end through a crushing defeat for the Teutonic Knights, was 'le bastard d'Escoce, qui se appelloit comte de Hembe', the nature of whose illegitimate provenance has not yet been identified. Nor has it yet been proven that any of the Scots involved in the campaigns before Tannenberg actually penetrated as far as lands attached to the Grand Duchy of Muscovy, although the probability must be strong.[1]

Equally, as that Grand Duchy consolidated and increased its territories throughout the 15th century, almost certainly there were representatives of the far-flung Scottish nation playing a part in promoting or resisting that process. However, the first such person known definitely to have been in Muscovy was 'Master David', an ambassador sent by King Christian I of Denmark to Tsar Ivan III in or around the year 1495. This ambassador was identified by an historian of the early years of the University of Copenhagen as 'Petrus Davidis de Scotia Aberdonensis'. It seems that this Peter Davidson was first brought to Copenhagen in 1479 to help develop the new university. He was a Master of the Sorbonne in Paris, and must have left his native town well before the foundation of its own first university, later known as King's College, in 1495, the almost certain year of his embassy to Muscovy. A few years later, in 1507, four Scottish metalworkers whose speciality was artillery were ordered to go to Moscow by the then King of Denmark, Johann, nephew of the Scottish King James IV.[2]

After 1507, there is again a frustrating silence from the sources until the middle of the 16th century. Then, in 1553, the English explorer, Richard Chancellor, stopped off in Norway en route for an attempt to discover a North-East Passage to the Indies. In Norway:

it happened that he fell in company and speech with certain Scottishmen who, having understanding of his intentions and wishing well to his actions, began earnestly to dissuade him from the further prosecution of the discovery by amplifying the dangers which he was to fall into and omitted no reason that might serve to that purpose.

These knowledgeable words of advice proved to be all too well founded as the expedition involving Chancellor rounded the Northern Cape only to meet disaster in the White Sea. Chancellor himself survived, and reached the court of Moscow, where he had audience with Tsar Ivan IV, better known as the Terrible. On his return journey, Chancellor was accompanied by a Russian ambassador, Osip Nepea. Again, there was disaster, a shipwreck on the Scottish coast near Fraserburgh. Chancellor perished while Nepea was spared, but lost the gifts that he was taking to the court in London. As Hakluyt put it, after the ship broke up in a bay named 'Pettislego', 'the mass and body of the goods laden in her, was by the rude and ravenous people of the country thereunto adjoining, rifled, spoiled, and carried away....

Nepea struggled through to London in 1556, and in the following year went back to Moscow with another English expedition. Contacts between England and Scotland and Muscovite Russia now became more frequent, and an agent of the Russia Company, Sir Jerome Horsey, provided some interesting information about Scots entering Muscovy in a less voluntary manner. Describing Ivan the Terrible's struggle for a foothold on the Baltic Sea in 1581, Horsey wrote:

The emperor's soldiers and army, far greater in number, ranged far into the Swedes' country and did much spoil and rapine, brought many captives away to remote places in his land, Livonians, French, Scots, Dutchmen, and some English. The emperor settling and seating a great many of them in the city of Moscow to inhabit by themselves without the city....

Here were the beginnings of the Foreign Settlement or German Quarter in which many Scots and other immigrants

An extract from the *Nikonian Chronicle* showing (from top to bottom) Ivan IV seeing off his ambassador Nepea; Chancellor's drowning during the shipwreck in Pitsligo Bay; and Nepea's eventual arrival in London.

were to live down to the end of the 17th century. According to Horsey, 'among other nations, there were four score and five poor Scots soldiers left of seven hundred sent from Stockholm, and three Englishmen in their company, brought among other captives in most miserable manner piteous to behold'. Horsey claimed that he interceded with the 'emperor' Ivan the Terrible on behalf of the Scots, and managed to find useful employment for them on the campaigns which took place usually for three months each summer against the Crimean Tatars. This is how Horsey described the process, beginning with his description of how the Scottish prisoners differed from the Swedes, Poles and Livonians, his enemies:

They were a nation strangers, remote, adventurous, and warlike people, ready to serve any Christian prince for maintenance and pay, as they would appear and prove if it pleased his majesty to employ and spare them such maintenance, now out of heart and clothes and arms, as they may show themselves and valor against his mortal enemy the Krym Tatar. It seems some use was made of this advice, for shortly the best soldiers and men-at-arms of these strangers were spared and put apart, and captains of each nation appointed to govern the rest—Jamy Lingett for the Scottish men, a valiant honest man. Money, clothes and daily allowance for meat and drink was given them, horse, hay, and oats; swords, piece, and pistols were they armed with. Poor snakes afore, look now cheerfully. Twelve hundred of them did better service against the Tatar than twelve thousand Russes with their short bow and arrows. The Krym, not knowing then the use of piece and pistols, struck dead off their horses with shot they saw not, cried, 'Away with those new devils that come with their thundering puffs,' whereat the emperor made good sport. Then had they pensions and lands allowed them to live upon, married and matched with the fair Livonian women, increased into families and live in favor of the prince and people.[3]

Horsey's facts and figures are notoriously unreliable, but there seems to be at least some element of reality in his description of the activities of Scottish soldiers in Muscovy during the reign of Ivan the Terrible. The identity of 'Jamy Lingett' remains elusive, and we know the names of few of his contemporaries. Perhaps the most successful of them was a

Sir Jerome Horsey depicted on a visit to the Scots quarter in Moscow.

General Carmichael, who in 1570 was made commander of 5,000 men in a war against Poland, and who later became Governor of the city of Pskov. He was probably the uncle of Sir John Carmichael, Warden of the Border, of the Hyndford family. Horsey mentions one Gabriel Elphinstone, 'a valiant Scottish captain', who came in with six fellow-countrymen to serve in Muscovy on the recommendation of a Colonel Steward who had served the King of Denmark. And a 17th-century English immigrant, Dr Samuel Collins, told the following story of an incident at Ivan the Terrible's court:

Some foreigners, English and Scots, had laughed at certain things the Tsar had done during a drinking bout. The Tsar when he heard this had them stripped naked and forced them to pick up, one by one, five or six bushels of peas which had been poured into his room. Then he gave them drink and sent them away.[4]

Soon after the death of Ivan the Terrible, there ensued, at the end of the 16th century, a turbulent period of Russian history later known as the Dark Time or the Time of Troubles, with aspects of which many of us have made acquaintance by way of Mussorgsky's opera, *Boris Godunov*. Among Scottish soldiers making their mark in the reign of Tsar Boris was a Captain David Gilbert, who was at first in that Tsar's entourage but then moved over to join the bodyguard of his usurper, the first false Dmitrii. According to Dr Collins, this bodyguard was composed of three hundred foreigners, divided into English, French and Scottish squadrons, each commanded by an officer of the appropriate nation. Gilbert later fought for the invading Poles, but was captured and brought to Moscow. He was the subject of a complaint made to James VI and I in 1617 by Tsar Michael Romanov, whose accession in 1613 had brought the Time of Troubles to an end. James interceded on Gilbert's behalf, with apparent success. Among other Scots known to have been involved in the struggles of the Time of Troubles were Robert Carr, Robert Dunbar and Thomas Gilbert, son of David. More anonymous were the Scots who formed part of an invading Swedish army in 1610.

Among 445 foreign officers in Russian service in 1624, there are known to be a Leslie, a Keith and a Matthison, but, like their predecessors, they remain shadowy figures. It is not until after 1630 that we can find more detailed information, and even then, most of the Scottish soldiers remain names only. According to a pre-revolutionary Russian military historian, it was in 1630 that Tsar Michael Romanov's government decided to form regiments on the European model with foreigners in charge as commanders and instructors. A decree of that year ordered all foreigners of the old and new emigration, that is before and after 1613, whether landed or not, to come to Moscow for service under two colonels, the Swiss Frantz Petsner and the Scot Alexander Leslie. This Leslie had just been sent by the Swedish King Gustavus Adolphus to promote Russian enthusiasm for a war against Poland, in order that he could invade Europe from the north with at least one flank secure. It is unlikely, therefore, that he was the Leslie appearing in the list of 1624. The Matthison also in that list could have been George Mathesone, Mattison or Matthison, who, as Colonel in service of the Great Emperor of All Russia, in Moscow and ready to go to the wars with his regiment against the Emperor's enemies, made a last will and testament in the summer of 1633.[5]

If clothes make the man, we can make the fairly close acquaintance of this Scottish soldier. In the list of his possessions were a red satin kaftan and breeches, and a green damask kaftan and breeches, along with other garments made of silk and of just plain cloth. Mathesone, as the name is usually spelt in the document, owned a pair of embroidered gloves, two beaver hats, ten pairs of cuffs, two nightcaps and a looking glass. In addition to a couple of rapiers and a Russian sabre, he had seven books. Among those to whom he bequeathed his money and goods were his fellow officers Robert Humes and Alexander Gordon, and his relations back in Broughton near Edinburgh, the children of his uncle John, failing whom his uncle James. Another will made in the summer of 1632 by a Captain James Wahobb, very sick and weak, included among its items an 'old grey Scottish cloak' and some 'aqua vitae'. We also have promissory notes made in 1633 by Captain Thomas Lindsey of Leith and Captain James Murray, the latter in camp near Smolensk.[6]

A page from the will made in 1633 by Colonel George Mathesone in which he lists his possessions.

The recapture of this city was the principal aim of the war embarked upon by Muscovite Russia against Poland. Among other Scottish soldiers involved in it were William Kit or Keith, possibly the Keith from the list of 1624, Jacob Shaw and James Wartle. Letters of recommendation from Charles I to Tsar Michael were written in 1632 on behalf of, among others, James Bannatine, David Lesley and Thomas Lindsey.[7] Undoubtedly, however, the most prominent Scot in the War for Smolensk of 1632-34 was the aforementioned Alexander Lesley or Leslie, not to be confused with the bearer of the same name who later became the Earl of Leven. Like many contemporaries, including his namesake, Alexander Leslie (often referred to as Sir Alexander Leslie of Auchintoul—although neither his knighthood nor his association with Auchintoul can be proven) served in many different campaigns for several different masters. In his particular case, he had fought for both Poles and Swedes. His first contact with the Russians, if not earlier during the Time of Troubles, had been in 1618 when he had been taken prisoner along with some other Polish soldiers during the siege of Smolensk by the Poles. He was taken to Moscow where he was fortunate enough to get in touch with some of the foreign residents who stood surety for his parole until he was included in an exchange of prisoners. In 1626, he became a colonel in the Swedish army, and in 1629, he was first sent to Moscow by the Swedish King.

After a formal release from Swedish service, Leslie was sent to Moscow a second time by Gustavus Adolphus at the beginning of 1630, and began to organize modern regiments. A year later, he was ordered to go abroad to hire up to five thousand men, to buy ten thousand muskets and five thousand swords. Several of those eventually engaged were Scots, and some were English. During the ensuing unsuccessful siege of Smolensk by the Russian forces, there were disputes between the old British enemies, and Leslie shot an English officer Thomas Sanderson. The exact details of the incident are difficult to establish. However, once again, Leslie was able to avoid condemnation and even a trial through the intercession of members of the Muscovy Company, who made him one of their own number.

Leslie was thus enabled to leave Muscovy, but he soon returned. In March 1637, Charles I wrote a letter of recommendation to Tsar Michael on his behalf, and he himself wrote to Michael from Narva, just beyond the frontier, in July 1638, a letter warning of the formation of a new Polish knightly order, and the consequent threat to the Orthodox Tsar and his people posed by the various papist vows taken by these potential crusaders. Leslie was soon back in Russian service, and indeed was to become naturalised. In the reign of Michael's son and successor, Alexis, Leslie's wife offended the peasants on their estate near the Volga by throwing an icon on the fire, and the couple escaped the consequences of this sacrilegious act by embracing Orthodoxy and Russian nationality. There are still Leslies living in the Soviet Union today, descending from Alexander or one of the other members of the family known to be in Russian service.[8]

Perhaps the most famous of the Scottish soldiers involved in the Thirty Years War from 1618 to 1648 has been Sir Walter Scott's fictional creation, 'Sir Dugald Dalgetty of Drumthwacket'. That knight introduces himself at the beginning of *A Legend of Montrose* with a brief autobiography:

My father, my lord, having by unthrifty courses reduced a fair patrimony to a non-entity, I had no better shift, when I was eighteen years old, than to carry the learning whilk I had acquired at the Mareschal-College of Aberdeen, my gentle bluid and designation of Drumthwacket, together with a pair of stalwart arms, and legs conform, to the German wars, there to push my way as a cavalier of fortune. My lord, my legs and arms stood me in more stead than either my gentle kin, or my book-lear, and I found myself trailing a pike as a private gentleman under old Sir Ludovick Leslie, where I learned the rules of service so tightly, that I will not forget them in a hurry. Sir, I have been made to stand guard eight hours, being from twelve at noon to eight o' clock of the night, at the palace, armed with back and breast, headpiece and bracelets, being iron to the teeth, in a bitter frost, and the ice was as hard as ever was flint: and all for stopping an instant to speak to my landlady, when I should have gone to the roll-call.

In an introduction to his novel written in 1829, Sir Walter commented:

The author has endeavoured to enliven the tragedy of the tale by the introduction of a personage proper to the time and country. In this he has been held by excellent judges to have been in some degree successful. The contempt of commerce entertained by young men having some pretence to gentility, the poverty of the country of Scotland, the national disposition to wandering and adventure, all conduced to lead the Scots abroad into the military service of countries which were at war with each other. They were distinguished on the continent by their bravery; but in adopting the trade of mercenary soldiers, they necessarily injured their national character. The tincture of learning, which most of them possessed, degenerated into pedantry; their good breeding became mere ceremonial; their fear of dishonour no longer kept them aloof from that which was really unworthy, but was made to depend on certain punctilious observances totally apart from that which was in itself deserving of praise. A cavalier of honour, in search of his fortune, might, for example, change his service as he would his shirt, fight, like the doughty Captain Dalgetty, in one cause or another, without regard to the justice of the quarrel, and might plunder the peasantry subjected to him by the fate of war with the most unrelenting rapacity; but he must beware how he sustained the slightest reproach, even from a clergyman, if it had regard to neglect on the score of duty.

Sir Walter's archetype, although in many ways skilfully drawn from the real lives of Scottish mercenaries whose careers he had studied, was arguably too critical. It is by no means certain that all the soldiers were contemptuous of commerce. We have already seen how, on at least two occasions, one of them, Alexander Leslie, made use of connexions with such civilian emigrants to effect his safety from imprisonment and trial in Muscovy. Secondly, national character and mercenary activity were far from incompatible in the circumstances of the 17th century, however abhorrent such plying for military hire might have become by the 19th century. Thirdly, the 'tincture of learning' by no means always degenerated into pedantry, nor the sense of honour into punctiliousness. As for plunder of the peasantry, that was another practice of the times widely accepted by soldier and civilian alike (if not, of course, by the peasantry which formed the bulk of the population through-

The Foreign Hostelry in Moscow where many Scots stayed.

out Europe). Finally, motives for turning mercenary could be religious, either fervour for the Protestant cause on the continent or the realization that there was not much future for Roman Catholicism in Scotland.

Of course, mercenary activity was engaged in by definition for rewards, which in 17th-century Muscovy could be various. Immigrant soldiers would normally receive a combination of three kinds of payment: a gratuity or gift at the time of arrival or departure; provision for subsistence and more valuable items such as furs and jewels; money and/or land. Those such as Alexander Leslie who converted to Orthodoxy would receive additional gifts. On that occasion, Leslie was given various items of rich apparel, including shirts, belts and gloves, kaftans, breeches and boots, and hats. He was also presented with several lengths of velvet and other expensive cloths, and eighty sables, together with a golden crucifix inset with a precious stone. Altogether, the value of the items received by Leslie and his family has been calculated at nearly 1,400 rubles, that is about 700 pounds sterling at the rate of exchange then in operation. Moreover, he received a considerable amount of land, an annual salary and a monthly subsistence allowance.[9]

Leslie was not alone in Muscovy during the period following the Smolensk War. In 1636, a 'Colonel John Kynninmonth, Governor of Nettenburg in Russia', whose family also had a branch in Sweden, was given permission by the Privy Council of Scotland to have a 'Certificate of his lawful birth and progeny...exped under the Great Seal'. Other British officers were in charge of regiments in other provincial cities such as Tula and Belgorod. One of them, Alexander Crawford, was ordered by Tsar Michael in 1639 to undertake the task of instructing the *streltsy* or musketeers in foreign modes of drill.[10] The *streltsy* themselves were reluctant to undergo such discipline, showing signs of an unrest that flared up throughout the 17th century, but the Tsar was insistent and Crawford duly carried out his assignment.

Soon after the death of Michael and the accession of his young son Alexis in 1645, relations between Muscovy and the British government deteriorated, especially with the execution of Charles I, which persuaded Alexis to banish from Muscovy English merchants in particular. Then, in 1650, there appeared in the Low Countries a publication entitled *A Declaration, of his Imperiall Majestie, the most High and Mighty Potentate Alexea, Emperor of Russia and Great-Duke of Muscovia*, protesting against the murder of Charles I and calling upon all Christian princes to come to a general diet in Antwerp to make arrangements for a holy war against the regicides. This was obviously a forgery by royalist sympathizers and might well have been the work of Lord Culpepper, who returned to France via Holland from Moscow in 1650 after a mission to the Russian capital on behalf of Charles II. Alexis does not appear to have taken offence at this forgery, but rather to have continued and developed the friendship between the Romanovs and Stuarts.[11]

In 1655, two of the leading adherents to the Stuart cause came to Muscovy. Thomas Dalyell of the Binns and William Drummond of 'Cromlix', both of whom had managed to escape from imprisonment by Parliament to the continent, received the support of Charles II to pursue their careers further afield. The exiled king gave each of them a safe-conduct pass for themselves, their families and retinues, pointing out that both soldiers were keen to serve some other monarch. In 1656, Charles wrote direct to Alexis on behalf of Dalyell, who, said the king, had 'served us so gallantly and so faithfully against our rebellious Subjects and hath performed so many actions of valour, prudence, and experience in Martial affairs. Drummond accompanied Dalyell to Moscow in the summer of 1656, and both of them remained in Alexis's service until the beginning of 1665. Although they duly performed various assignments, they were also both of somewhat turbulent disposition. A Danish visitor to Muscovy in 1659 told the following story about Drummond, who decided to punish a merchant named Karl Kohl for insulting him and his fellow Scots. Drummond invited Kohl to his house, where he himself, along with a Colonel Johnston who had come to Moscow at the same time, and with others, assaulted the unsuspecting merchant. They placed a cocked pistol against his head, and threatened to shoot him if he put up a struggle or cried out for help. Then they cut the coat off his back, bound and gagged him, and ordered one of Drummond's servants to whip him soundly. On his release, Kohl took Drummond to court, where he was fined and obliged to ask Kohl's pardon. Moreover, the story concludes, if there had not been a great need for officers at that time, the Tsar would have ordered Drummond's right arm and both ears to be cut off. Generally speaking, the Scottish mercenaries had a reputation for unruliness, some examples of which we have already noted. A contemporary of Drummond and Dalyell, a Colonel James Main, was exiled to Siberia for some grave offence, probably for fighting a duel. These and other such incidents helped to bring about a Muscovite saying that the British immigrants as a whole 'are not avaricious, but they love to squabble'.

Dalyell and Drummond experienced some difficulty in leaving Muscovy by early 1665, and needed the intercession of the restored Charles II before they were able to make their departure. Yet, in the end, they left with honour, as was shown in the patent granted to Dalyell by 'Our Czarian Majesty to the great sovereign Kings, to the Ministers of State, Dukes, Counts and to all free Gentlemen whom it may concern':

…Thomas Dalyell Lieutenant General, formerly came over hither, in order to serve our Great Czarian Majesty, and whilst he was with us in our dominions, he did serve our great Sovereign and Czarian Majesty: He stood against our Enemies, and fought valiantly. The Military Men, that were under his Command, he regulated, disciplined, and led them to Battle himself: and he did and performed everything faithfully as becoming a noble Commander. And for these faithful services, we the great Lord and Czarian Majesty were pleased to order the said Lieutenant General to be a General, He being worthy of that Honour through his Merit.

The patent stated that Dalyell would be welcome back for further service at any time, and guaranteed his further departure.

Their years in Muscovy enhanced the reputation of both Dalyell and Drummond for severity. Sir John Lauder, the distinguished lawyer, observed in 1684 about the use of thumb-screws for torture that 'the authors of this invention of

Portrait of General Tam Dalyell at the House of the Binns. (By permission of the National Trust for Scotland.)

the thummikins were General Dalyell and Drummond, who had seen it in Moscovia'. However, he added, 'it is also used among our coilyiars in Scotland, and is called the pilliwincks'. Lauder also recorded popular murmurs against the 'Muscovian rigour' of Dalyell's military administration back in Scotland. He related how a Covenanter, brought before a committee of the Privy Council, denounced its members as 'bloody murderers and papists' and described Dalyell as 'a Muscovia beast who used to roast men'. The Covenanter Kirkton characterized Dalyell as a man whose 'rude and fierce natural disposition had been much confirmed by his breeding and service in Muscovia, where he had the command of a small army, and saw nothing but tyranny and slavery'. Bishop Burnet wrote of Drummond that 'he had yet too much of the air of Russia about him, though not with Dalyell's fierceness'. 'Old Tom of Muscovy', as Dalyell was often called, died in Edinburgh in August 1685. Drummond was created Viscount of Strathallan in 1686, and died two years later. Both of them had laboured as hard for the Stuart cause back in Scotland as they had for that of the Romanovs in faraway Muscovy.[12]

There, at about the same time as the restoration of Charles II, Alexis had decided that he needed to recruit more western officers as part of his drive to consolidate Muscovy's position against a series of enemies, actual and potential, ranging from the Crimean Tartars through the Poles to the Swedes. Among the recruits was another batch of Scotsmen, including John Hamilton, William Hay, Paul Menzies and the most renowned of them all, Patrick Gordon. These new arrivals certainly became acquainted with Dalyell and Drummond, while according to some accounts, they met the aged Alexander Leslie, who preceded those two fellow-countrymen as Governor of the frontier town of Smolensk, with which he had so many connexions throughout his career.

Times were now changing, and Muscovite Russia was necessarily opening itself up to more influences from the West, without which it could not hope to guarantee its survival in an increasingly competitive world. Diplomatic contacts with other states in Europe were developing, and cultural adaptations were taking place in Muscovy itself. In these areas, as well as in the more purely military sphere, the Scots were making a significant contribution. Paul Menzies, who came from an old Aberdonian Roman Catholic family, rose quickly through the commissioned ranks of the regular regiments of the army and was soon entrusted with important missions abroad. Most notably, in the summer of 1672, he was sent off to Rome in order to attempt to improve relations between Tsar and Pope. Possibly, a new crusade could be agreed against the Crimean Tatars and their more formidable patrons, the Ottoman Turks. Unfortunately, negotiations were crippled by disputes over protocol. On his return to Moscow in 1674, Menzies served for a further twenty years before his death at the end of 1694. His elaborate funeral was among the many interesting incidents described in the diary of Patrick Gordon.[13]

This is by far the fullest source that we possess concerning the activities of Scottish soldiers in Muscovy. Through it, we achieve much of our understanding of both these mercenaries and the environment in which they performed their duties. The first part of the diary concerns Gordon's early career before his arrival in Moscow in September 1661. Born on Easter Tuesday 31 March 1635, at his father's estate of Easter Auchleuchries, near the small town of Ellon sixteen miles or so to the north of Aberdeen, Gordon 'attained to as much learning as the ordinary country schools afford'. Leaving school in 1651, he left Aberdeen for a variety of reasons (including his Roman Catholicism, an unhappy love affair, the assumed pressure of parental constraints, his junior position in the house of Gordon—the younger son of a younger brother of a minor branch of the family). Accident rather than design took him across the sea to Danzig via Elsinore in Denmark. Gordon at first continued his education for a couple of years or so at the Jesuit College of Braunsberg, near Königsberg. Then he drifted into the life of a soldier, rather than positively choosing it, and spent the years from 1653 to 1661 in learning the tools and methods of this trade in Swedish and Polish service. In 1661, he decided to enter Russian service, attracted by the promise of better conditions and more certain pay, and travelled to the Russian capital with his above-mentioned fellow-

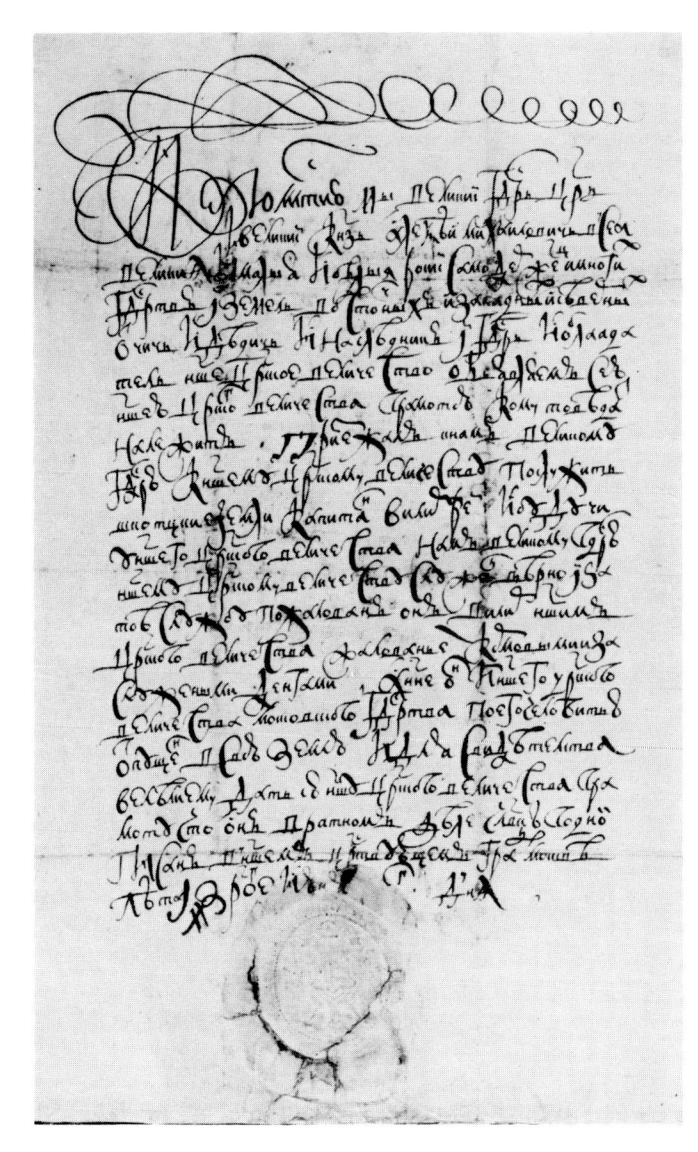

A charter of 1667 from Tsar Aleksei Mikhailovich attesting to the military capability of a Scottish captain Vilirres [Villiers?], who had served in his army and was now returning home.

countrymen. Gordon lamented his decision to come to Moscow and took a dim view of its inhabitants:

…the people being morose, avaricious, deceitful, false, insolent and tyrannous when they have command, and being under command, submissive and even slavish, sloven and base, and yet overweening and valuing themselves above all other nations.…

The conditions of service, especially problems concerning pay, and many more other personal reasons, including an abiding interest in the family estates back at Auchleuchries, were only too sufficient to persuade him to think of leaving Russia if and when possible. But in the short run, he soon discovered that he would be allowed to leave Moscow only for exile in Siberia, and in the longer run, there were a whole series of further complications. And so, he was to remain in the service of the Tsars for thirty-eight years, with no more than a few visits back home. These enabled him to keep in touch with family affairs, and also abreast of the latest political, military and cultural developments.

The first of these visits was in 1666, five years after his arrival in Moscow. He was delayed in Bruges, and wrote a letter seeking intercession by the Secretary of State for Scotland, the Earl of Lauderdale. When he finally reached London, Gordon was able to transact the business of the mission on which he had been sent, involving the improvement of relations with Charles II. He met the King himself, Lauderdale and many other high-placed officials. Some time after his return to Moscow, in 1668, he sent Lauderdale a letter of gratitude couched in high-flown terms, along with a token of respect consisting of 'a piece of unsophisticated caviar in its mother's skin which will make a cup of good liquor taste the better, and hath besides an extraordinary strengthening quality'.

The Scottish officer also informed the Scottish Secretary that he was soon to leave Moscow with his regiment on a campaign against the Cossacks and Tatars to the south. He probably remained there for most of the next ten years, although we know that he made another visit to England and this time Scotland, too, in the years 1669 and 1670. We have a letter of his, dated 12 October 1669, from Edinburgh to

London, to a Joseph Williamson, Secretary to Lord Arlington, a member of the entourage of Charles II, observing that:

> ...I go into the country to my parents where wintering, I intend to return to Russia in the spring and hoped to go by the way of Poland. If in this journey I find no grounds for a settlement anywhere else, I intend to continue in Russia sometime longer, albeit God knoweth the pay there yields us but a very bare subsistence as things go now. Even in Scotland soldiers of fortune can attain no honourable employment for nobles and persons of great quality. In England aliens are seldom employed, so that necessity (who was never yet a good pilot) constrained us to serve foreign princes when notwithstanding if with honour we could be any ways steadable to our native country it would be some comfort....

Gordon's remarks could have been made by many other Scottish soldiers in Muscovy. As for himself, he gained honour if not employment in Scotland when he was made a burgess of Aberdeen on 6 May 1670. Immediately on his return to Russia, he discovered that his pay had been cut to a third of its former level, and petitioned for dismissal from the Tsar's service. But this was not granted then or later, in spite of many efforts to achieve it. The Scottish exile made one more visit to his homeland, in 1686, when he renewed and developed contacts in Aberdeen, Edinburgh and London, where James VII and II showed great interest in him. For a short time, it looked as if Gordon might change the Romanov master for the Stuart, but it was not to be.

Gordon maintained his contacts through an energetic correspondence, which also enabled him to keep up interests far transcending those of his basic profession of mercenary soldier. From 1691 to 1692 for example, he sent letters to London asking for books to be sent to him on a wide range of subjects including history, the law, medicine, chivalric writings, the classics, and leisure activities as well as military matters. In the Foreign Settlement, these books would no doubt be read and discussed over dinner and at play (especially bowls). But activities there were not always so peaceful: in a restricted area, tempers could fray, and the mercenaries on several occasions took recourse to the off-duty use of their weapons of war in duels. We have already encountered some examples of such bickering. Gordon himself had become involved in a duel five years after his arrival in Moscow, when he invited 'his Sacred Majesty's subjects of the best quality' to celebrate the birthday of Charles II on 29 May 1666, when:

> ...we were all very merry till after dinner Major Montgomery and I got a quarrel, he being much in wrong and very injurious to me which not to disturb the company upon such a day I passed, and we promised to meet the next day and decide it by duel on horse-back.

In fact, before the encounter could take place, some English merchants persuaded the intending participants to patch up their quarrel. This was just as well for Gordon, who might well otherwise have been refused permission to make his impending visit back to Britain.

A more recurrent theme in the diary than such quarrels reflected the Roman Catholicism of Gordon and other inhabitants of the Foreign Settlement, including several fellow Scots. On 31 January 1684, in conference with the leading adviser to the Regent Sophia, V. V. Golitsyn, Gordon complained that Roman Catholics had no free exercise of religion such as enjoyed by others. Golitsyn told him that they should petition the two young joint Tsars, Ivan and Peter, and permission would be granted. So duly, Gordon and his co-religionists submitted their request:

> ...We, your servants, serve you Great Sovereigns and labour for you for many years in good faith and truth, and we merchants live by your, the Great Sovereigns' ukaze, and we live in the Foreign Settlement, and we your servants are on duty in different towns, and we have no house of prayer and no priest for our souls. And, O Sovereigns, those foreigners who are of the Lutheran and Calvinist faith have priests and houses of prayer, whereas we have no purification in faith, and we suffer therefrom great damage to our souls. Charitable Sovereigns, Tsars and Grand Dukes, Ivan Alekseevich and Peter Alekseevich, Autocrats of all Great and Little and White Russia, be good to us, your servants, and to us, merchants, and order, O Sovereigns, for the salvation of our souls, to call in priests and also to entertain a house of prayer, as have the Lutherans and Calvinists, and to deliver for this, your Great Sovereigns', letters patent.

General Patrick Gordon.

On 11 August 1684, Gordon recorded that permission had been obtained from their Majesties at the intercession of the Ambassador of the Holy Roman Emperor to build a church and to maintain priests. No doubt, the petition submitted by Gordon, Paul Menzies, David William de Graham, Alexander Leviston and others had also made some impact. Soon after this, a wooden Roman Catholic Church was built in Moscow, and in 1695, a stone replacement. Gordon's fear that he would die unshriven in the wilds of Muscovy need not now be realized.[14]

Gordon departed this life on 29 November 1699, at the age of sixty-four. Therefore, he did not live to see even the beginning of the Northern War against Sweden that would transform Muscovy into the Russian Empire. The young Tsar whom he had advised throughout the 1690s rose by means of this war from obscurity to wide fame as Peter the Great. Now the necessity for foreign mercenaries was no longer compelling, as the Russian army could stand on its own feet. True, the junior service—the navy—would need foreign tutelage for some time to come. Scots would continue to serve in the Navy and the Army too, some with great distinction. Thomas Gordon became an Admiral during the reign of Peter the Great, James Keith rose to high military rank in the 1730s and 1740s after Peter's death, before leaving for more distinction as Marshal to Frederick the Great of Prussia. And so on. By the 18th century, some of the Scottish families had been in Russia long enough to have become completely russified. So it was with branches of the Bruce and Hamilton, as well as the Gordon and Leslie families, for example. Although a minority, including Dalyell and Drummond, had been able to return to pursue their careers back in Scotland, generally speaking, the impact of these mercenaries on their homeland was small.

But on Muscovy, especially in the 17th century, there can be little doubt that their influence was considerable. Individual contributions such as those of Alexander Leslie and Patrick Gordon were enormous. Their less celebrated fellow-countrymen played a significant part in the training of modern regiments and in the series of wars that Muscovy fought against Poles and Swedes, Ottoman Turks and Crimean Tatars. Moreover, as we have seen, their activity was by no means exclusively military, but diplomatic and cultural, too. It would, of course, be going too far to suggest that Muscovy would not have been transformed into the Russian Empire without the contribution of the Scottish soldiers. But perhaps it is not an exaggeration to assert that they helped to ensure that such a transformation was well under way by the end of the 17th century.

NOTES

1. The introductory material is based on Alan Macquarrie, *Scotland and the Crusades, 1095-1560*, Edinburgh, 1985, pp. 83-8.
2. William Keith Leask, ed., *Musa Latina Aberdonensis*, New Spalding Club, Aberdeen, 1892-1910, III, xvi-xviii; J. W. Barnhill and Paul Dukes, 'North-East Scots in Muscovy in the Seventeenth Century', *Northern Scotland*, 1(1972), 50.
3. Chancellor and Horsey quotations from Lloyd E. Berry and Robert O. Crummey, eds, *Rude and Barbarous Kingdom: Russia in the Accounts of Sixteenth-Century English Voyagers*, London, 1968, pp. 17, 288-9.
4. Information on Carmichael and Elphinstone, as well as Collins quotation, from A. Francis Steuart, *Scottish Influences in Russian History: From the End of the Sixteenth Century to the Beginning of the Nineteenth Century*, Edinburgh, 1913, pp. 17-20.
5. Steuart, *Scottish Influences*, p. 32.
6. Bonds and Papers of the Ashe Family, Suffolk Record Office, S1/1/77,6,9.
7. Geraldine Marie Phipps, *Britons in Seventeenth-Century Russia: A Study in the Origins of Modernization*, University of Pennsylvania PhD Dissertation (University Microfilms, Ann Arbor, Michigan, 1972), pp. 269-70, 282, 319; Steuart, *Scottish Influences*, pp. 40-1.
8. Paul Dukes, 'The Leslie Family in the Swedish Period (1630-5) of the Thirty Years' War', *European Studies Review*, xii(4), 401-24.
9. Vasily Storozhev, *Podarki Tsaria Alekseeia polkovniku Lesli dlia kreshcheniia i za podnachalstvo 1625g*, Moscow, 1895, pp. 1-6.
10. Steuart, *Scottish Influences*, p. 40; Phipps, *Britons*, pp. 321, 324.
11. Barnhill and Dukes, 'North-East Scots', p. 54.
12. Paul Dukes, 'Problems concerning the Departure of Scottish Soldiers from Seventeenth-Century Muscovy', in T. C. Smout, ed., *Scotland and Europe, 1200-1850*, Edinburgh, 1986, pp. 143-56; Phipps, *Britons*, 271-2, 306.
13. Paul Dukes, 'Paul Menzies and His Mission from Muscovy to Rome, 1672-1674', *The Innes Review*, xxxv (autumn 1984), 88-95.
14. The original of the Gordon Diary is in the Military Historical Archive, Moscow. Part of it has been published in Joseph Robertson, ed., *Passages from the Diary of General Patrick Gordon of Auchleuchries, 1635-1699* (The Spalding Club, Aberdeen, 1859). Some of the above material is taken from Paul Dukes, 'Aberdeen and North-East Scotland: Some Archival and Other Sources', in Janet M. Hartley ed., *The Study of Russian History from British Archival Sources*, London, 1986.

For brief illustrated articles on the Keiths, Leslies, Gordons and Menzies, see respectively the Aberdeen *Leopard* magazine, June-July 1986, December-January 1986-7, February-March 1987, and June-July 1987.

SCOTO-RUSSIAN CONTACTS IN THE REIGN OF CATHERINE THE GREAT (1762-1796)

A. G. CROSS

CATHERINE II's accession to the Russian throne in 1762 ushered in an epoch in Anglo-Russian relations that was unprecedented in its richness and variety and was not to be rivalled in the subsequent history of Imperial Russia. While it is not always possible or even meaningful to distinguish Scoto-Russian relations from Anglo-Russian at this period or any other, it is nonetheless true that contacts between Scotland and Russia flourished in new and significant ways. Scottish merchant houses participated in the general prospering of British trade with Russia, consolidated by new Anglo-Russian Commercial Agreements in 1766 and 1793. Increasing numbers of ships sailed the Baltic between Leith and St Petersburg, importing far more than was exported. Among the British merchants in St Petersburg Scots figured prominently: Walter Shairp was British Consul-General between 1776 and 1787, as was his son, Stephen, between 1796 and 1807; Richard Sutherland, born in St Petersburg to a Scottish shipbuilder, became a Court banker and a Baron of the Russian Empire. Scottish soldiers were less prominent than in earlier periods, but naval officers achieved even greater eminence under Catherine. The same could be said of Scottish doctors, as will be evident from another contribution to this publication. Russia's demand for technological expertise is reflected in the number of Scottish workmen and craftsmen willing to leave their homeland for a few years—or for ever. But perhaps the period is most remarkable for Russians visiting Scotland, particularly students, lured by the excellence of its universities and the fame of its scholars. Scottish scholars for their part reveal their interest in Russian affairs and Russia saw its first translations of a wide range of works by Scottish authors. Cultural, scientific and scholarly ties were further cemented by mutual elections to prestigious societies and clubs.

The following essay does not pretend to be a comprehensive survey of contacts in Catherine's reign. It concentrates on certain episodes and certain individuals, and then not in equal detail; but, on occasion, it extends its chronological limits to highlight careers that flourished after the demise of the great Catherine.

I

Scottish soldiers were found in Russia from the time of Ivan the Terrible, first, seemingly, as prisoners of war, then as mercenaries entering Russian service. When Peter the Great set about building a navy, Scots figured prominently among the British officers he attracted into his service. Scots occupied positions of authority in both the Russian army and navy in the first half of the 18th century and the *Scots Magazine* could write in 1739: 'We may surely be indulged to take a little rational pride, in finding no action of consequence performed in which Gentlemen of this nation are not in particular manner distinguished for their bravery and resolution: At the head of the Russian fleet we find a Gordon; in the highest rank of the army a Keith, and Douglas, Lesley, and many more, send their names from the extremities of that vast empire, and even from the inmost plains of Tartary'. The Russian army during Catherine's reign could boast of no Scottish officers of the stature of Field-Marshal James Keith, but the Russian navy was greatly indebted to the contribution of a number of outstanding Scots.

The efficient navy that Peter had built went into decline under his successors and Catherine at her accession had no illusions about its state. Following a review of the fleet at Kronshtadt in June 1765 she wrote: 'Nous avons des vaisseaux et du monde dessus à foison, mais nous n'avons ni flotte, ni mariniers... Il faut avouer, qu'ils ont l'air de la flotte pour la pêche des harengs, qui part d'Holland tous les ans, et non en vérité d'une flotte de guerre: pas un vaisseau ne tient son rang'. She had already begun to take steps to ameliorate the dismal situation by persuading the British government to accept a number of young Russians for training in the British navy and by recruiting experienced British officers. Between 1764 and 1772 over thirty British officers entered the Russian navy, some serving for only a short time, but others for the rest of their careers. The second great influx came in the 1780s when Anglo-Russian relations improved after the temporary cooling occasioned by the Armed Neutrality of 1780: no less than thirty-eight officers arrived in a body in 1783 and many more were recruited in the remaining years of Catherine's reign. By coincidence rather than by design the two periods of the most intensive recruitment occurred a few years before the Russian navy's involvement in its most important actions of the century, during the war against Turkey in 1769-73 and against Sweden in 1787-90 and the Turks again in 1787-92. These wars brought the spectacular naval victories against the Turks in the Mediterranean at Chesme Bay in June 1770 and against the Swedes at Hogland in July 1788. In both battles a significant percentage of the Russian ships were commanded by British officers, including Scots.

A number of Scottish officers recruited into the Russian navy before Catherine's accession continued to serve during her reign. Of these perhaps the most notable were Peter Anderson and Thomas Mackenzie who had both come to Russia in 1736. Anderson became a Vice-Admiral in 1769 in command of the Baltic fleet, but retired the following year; Mackenzie was promoted to Rear-Admiral in 1765 but died in 1766. It is another Thomas Mackenzie whose eminence belonged completely to Catherine's reign. Entering Russian service as a midshipman in 1765, Mackenzie commanded a fire-ship at Chesme and was successful in setting fire to a Turkish galley, from which the flames spread to the rest of the fleet. He was promoted to captain immediately after the battle. The *Scots Magazine* accompanied its report of the battle with two letters from Mackenzie, describing the action. By 1783 Mackenzie had risen to Rear-Admiral in the Black Sea Fleet, and he was responsible for directing the harbour installations at the new port of Sevastopol. It was in Sevastopol that he died in 1786 and a monument to his memory was erected on a hill overlooking the town. Another Scottish officer in charge of a fire-ship at Chesme was Robert Dugdale, who was also promoted to Rear-Admiral in 1783 and retired in 1790.

The highest-ranking British officer at Chesme was the Scot John Elphinston (1722-85), who entered Russian service in May 1769 and was made a Rear-Admiral in June. He commanded one of the three squadrons comprising the Russian fleet that sailed for the Mediterranean and clashed with Admiral Geary of the British navy at Portsmouth over protocol procedures. Elphinston was, indeed, a difficult and vain man, who was to come into conflict with the overall commander of the Russian fleet, Count Alexis Orlov, soon after Chesme: this led to his recall to St Petersburg and his dismissal from Russian service in 1771. Elphinston was undoubtedly a talented officer but one who preferred to command rather than obey. His contribution to the Chesme victory was considerable, but he was not the absolute architect he pretended to be or as he was depicted by a sympathetic fellow officer in *An Authentic Narrative of the Russian Expedition against the Turks*, published in London in 1772. Elphinston had two young sons serving with him in the Mediterranean. Although they resigned on their father's dismissal, one of them, Samuel, and another younger brother, Robert, were to join the Russian navy in 1783. Samuel died at the battle of Oland in 1789.

The first Scot to be admitted with the rank of Rear-Admiral was Charles Douglas in 1764, but he served for only a few months before rejoining the Royal Navy, where he also rose to be a Rear-Admiral and to receive a knighthood. Entering Russian service on the same day as Douglas were two kinsmen from Inverkeithing, William Roxburgh and Samuel

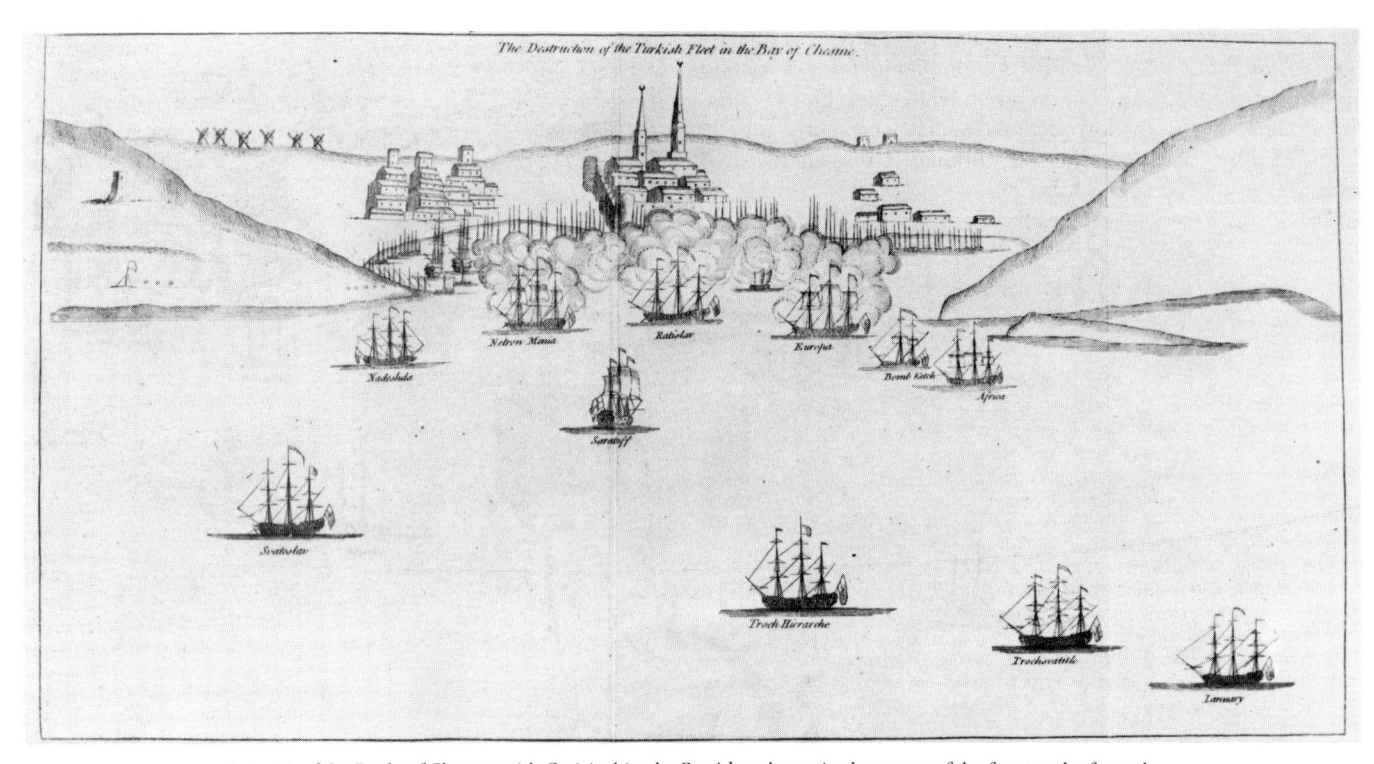

A sketch of the Battle of Chesme with Greig's ship, the *Rostislav*, shown in the centre of the front rank of vessels.

Greig. Roxburgh served at Chesme on Elphinston's flagship, which was afterwards wrecked, and throughout the rest of the Mediterranean campaign on the 66-gun *Vsevolod*. Although he achieved the rank of Rear-Admiral, he retired to Scotland the following year, when he disappears from view. This was far from the case with Greig (1735-88), who may justifiably be termed Catherine's most accomplished and devoted naval commander. He came to be admired by both British and Russian alike, and it would seem entirely appropriate to consider his career in some detail.

The museum of the Royal Burgh of Inverkeithing perpetuates the memory of the town's most famous son with a number of exhibits donated by a descendant of the admiral. They include most notably a copy of the portrait in oils by the Russian artist Ivan Petrovich Argunov from the 1770s and the dressing cabinet used by Greig aboard his ship, the *Rostislav*, during the Mediterranean campaign. It was at Chesme that Greig first came to prominence. He had left the Royal Navy as a master's mate, despite having served with distinction in a number of engagements, including Quiberon Bay in 1759 and the reduction of Havana in 1762. Greig entered the Russian navy as a Captain of the first rank. By the time he set sail for the Mediterranean, he was a Brigadier on board the 66-gun *Tri Ierarkha*, whose armament he had personally supervised the previous year. Early in 1770 Greig was detailed to fetch Count Orlov from Leghorn and the *Tri Ierarkha* became Orlov's flagship throughout 1770, which brought Greig into close and influential contact with his commander-in-chief. On 5-6 June there were fought the two actions which were subsequently known as the battle of Chesme, although Greig, in his own account of the events, terms the engagement during the morning and early afternoon of the first day the battle of Chios. The Turks were to retire after a brief but bloody battle to the mouth of the harbour of Chesme, where the second and decisive action was to be fought during the coming night, directed by Greig, who had transferred to the *Rostislav*. The Russian victory was complete, although, as has been suggested, the rivalry for the victor's laurels among the flag-captains was fierce. The official national hero was Orlov, whose alleged contribution was to be immortalised by the addition of a second barrel to his surname—Chesmenskii, but it is to Orlov's credit that he never attempted to minimize Greig's role, and the British Ambassador in St Petersburg, the Scot Lord Cathcart, wrote later that Greig 'has received every encomium courage and conduct could deserve'.

Greig proved himself not only courageous and capable, but loyal and discreet, and his career prospered accordingly. He was immediately promoted to Rear-Admiral and took part in many of the subsequent engagements in the Mediterranean. He returned briefly to Russia with his squadron before setting sail with his wife, Sarah (daughter of Alexander Cook, owner of a rope-walk at Kronshtadt) for Leghorn. Greig's final voyage home in 1775 is connected with the one incident which has cast a shadow on his otherwise unblemished career. Count Orlov brought to his flagship the unfortunate woman known as Princess Tarakanova, allegedly the daughter of the Empress Elizabeth by Count Razumovskii, and ordered Greig to sail for Russia with her as his prisoner. How much fore-knowledge Greig had of the affair is unclear, although he and his wife and the British consul at Leghorn, the Scot Sir John Dick and his wife certainly entertained Tarakanova and helped to allay any suspicions she might have had. Greig cannot be completely exonerated and the Tarakanova affair is further evidence of his

Admiral Samuel Greig.

devotion to the Empress Catherine, which was only put to the test when direct confrontation with Britain was involved.

A knight of the Orders of St George, 2nd class, and of St Anna with the completion of the Mediterranean campaign, Greig was soon the recipient of new honours: in July 1775 he was promoted to Vice-Admiral and appointed commandant of Kronshtadt; and a year later, on the occasion of Catherine's inspection of the Russian fleet, he received from her the ribbon of the order of St Alexander Nevskii. The year 1777 saw his triumphant return to Scotland and visit to England, where he was introduced to the King. Back in Edinburgh he received the freedom of the city. One further mark of esteem from Britain came in September 1781, when he was elected a Fellow of the Royal Society 'for many eminent Services in his Profession as well as for a very extensive knowledge in the various branches of Physics'. Finally, in 1782, Greig was raised to the rank of full Admiral.

Under Greig's supervision the port of Kronshtadt was subjected to a new facelift in the 1780s. The wooden linings of the docks were replaced with granite and a large granite mole was constructed. Kronshtadt was taking on that appearance of solid impregnability, considerably increased during the 19th century, which led a writer at the time of the Crimean War to remark that a 'Scotsman built those walls which years afterwards checked the career of his fellow-countryman Sir Charles Napier'. Greig's 'grand project' for Kronshtadt included the construction or reconstruction of the Admiralty, hospitals, the prison and the naval cadet college.

The Armed Neutrality of 1780 put British officers in Russian service in a difficult position, but Greig was not slow to make his position clear. The British Ambassador reported that he had been assured 'that if ever the Empress should require of them to serve in a manner hostile to us, they would, to a man, quit her service. Notwithstanding his high rank and lucrative post, I am sure he is sincere, as far as regards himself, and am happy to give this strong and undoubted testimonial of his character and principles.' Among several other incidents during the 1780s, when Greig's decisiveness and character were put to the test, mention might be made of the crisis occasioned in April 1788, when the arrival of John Paul Jones, 'the Scottish American', with the rank of Rear-Admiral in the Russian Navy, infuriated all the British officers, who promptly threatened to resign. It was only with great reluctance that Greig signed their petition to the Empress, but when it became clear that Catherine was not prepared to concede, he dissuaded his brother officers from further action. Russia had cause to be thankful to Greig, for it was involved in wars with Turkey and Sweden and had need of its British officers, who, indeed, were not found wanting. The war with Sweden was to take the lives of a number of British officers; it was also to take Greig's, although, ironically, not in combat.

Greig's war was to be a short one, a matter of a little over three months. During that period he fought the battle of Hogland, and blockaded the Swedes at Sveaborg. He had wrested the initiative from the Swedes, frustrated their plans to attack St Petersburg and captured the Swedish flagship at Hogland. Catherine's delight knew no bounds and Greig was made a knight of the order of St Vladimir, 1st class, and of St Andrew. But within weeks her joy turned to sincere grief, when she received news of Greig's death from fever on board his flagship at Revel on 26 October 1788. Catherine had a gold medal struck in his memory and ordered her architect Giacomo Quarenghi to prepare a design for his mausoleum. A state funeral was held in the Lutheran cathedral at Revel (now Tallinn) where he was buried. Despite her attempt to recruit a senior British officer she found no real successor to her trusted 'Strike Sure' Scottish admiral.

II

Some months before Greig's appointment as commandant of Kronshtadt, there arrived from Scotland a group of fourteen workmen under a chief engineer, Adam Smith. They had come to construct a 'fire-engine' or steam pump for the new dry docks at Kronshtadt, which was to become the wonder of the age and attract an endless stream of visitors, including Catherine herself in 1782. The first tests of the pump took place in 1777, at which time the majority of the workmen returned home, although Adam Smith remained to supervise the working of the machine and was joined in 1783 by his son, Alexander, who was himself a highly skilled engineer and produced a machine of his own design in 1792. The decision to order the original pump had been taken by the Russian government on the advice of Admiral Sir Charles Knowles, whom Catherine had invited into her service in 1770 to supervise ship-building and naval administration. Knowles had inspected Kronshtadt in 1773 and recommended replacing the antique windmills by steam pumps. An order was eventually placed with the famous Carron Company, where Charles Gascoigne, the Director, with the help of the engineer John Smeaton, produced a 'Grand Plan for converting the Mill N into a fire-engine for draining docks of Kronshtadt', but only after Knowles's secretary, John Robison, had made unsuccessful attempts to bring his acquaintance of Glasgow days, James Watt, to Russia.

The order for the fire-engine was not the Russian government's first dealings with Carron, nor its last. Its basic and continuing interest was in the techniques of cannon-founding and in workers with the required expertise. The Carron Company of Falkirk had begun the production of cannon in 1761, but it was only with the development of the Carronade naval gun from 1778 that its pre-eminence as an ordnance producer was assured. However, in 1772 the Russian Admiralty ordered one thousand tons of cannon from Carron and this arrived later that summer, preceded by a letter from Gascoigne to Admiral Knowles, expressing 'our Warm Wishes that under your Auspices: The Glory of Her Imperial Majesty's arms may be proclaimed from the mouths of our Artillery at the Gates of Constantinople'. Unfortunately, many of the cannon failed the severe Russian proof, and due to this and other internal factors the Russian government placed no further orders for more than a decade.

But there also came from Carron two expert cannon-founders. Although British law forbade the foreign recruitment of workmen, the Russian Ambassador in London contrived to sign on six-year contracts Adam Ramage and Joseph Powell in 1771. The two workers were sent off to the Lipetsk works near Voronezh, where Ramage was to die in 1775. Powell fully completed his contract and decided to return to Scotland. He changed his mind, however, and sought a new contract in order to demonstrate a new way of casting cannon. He was sent to the Aleksandrovsk foundry at Petrozavodsk, where his new method proved far from successful. Returning to St Petersburg in August 1778, Powell found the College of Mines still willing to employ him. He went again to Lipetsk and then ultimately to the Izhora iron-works near St Petersburg, where he died in 1789. But by this time the Russian government had succeeded in attracting from Carron a man of much greater expertise and authority, none other than its Director, Charles Gascoigne.

Greig's concern with the armament of the Russian fleet led him in the 1780s to turn once more to the Carron Company for quantities of cannon and for machinery; he also began to negotiate to secure the services of Gascoigne himself to 'établir une fonderie d'artillerie ici en Russie'. Gascoigne, beset by financial difficulties at home, eventually secured permission from the British government to emigrate despite considerable opposition from his associates. He arrived in Russia in May 1786, bringing with him machinery and a number of Carron workmen. For a time the British community in Russia seems to have ostracized both Gascoigne and Greig and lingering British hostility may be seen in an English visitor's description of him as an 'outlaw' as late as 1800.

Gascoigne, however, prospered in Russia, 'where he had a good income, lives in more splendour, and has greater connections than he can ever have in this country'. He was soon engaged in reorganizing after the Carron system the Aleksandrovsk works and the nearby Konchezersk foundry; in 1789 he set up a branch of the Petrozavodsk works at Kronshtadt on Kotlin Island, which was designed to make use of the old cannon there and to serve the immediate needs of the fleet. In the 1790s Gascoigne was asked to establish a new foundry at Lugansk in the south with the specific aim of supplying the needs of the Black Sea Fleet. This new foundry began production in 1797 during Paul's reign. Early in Alexander's reign, he reorganized the Admiralty's old Izhora

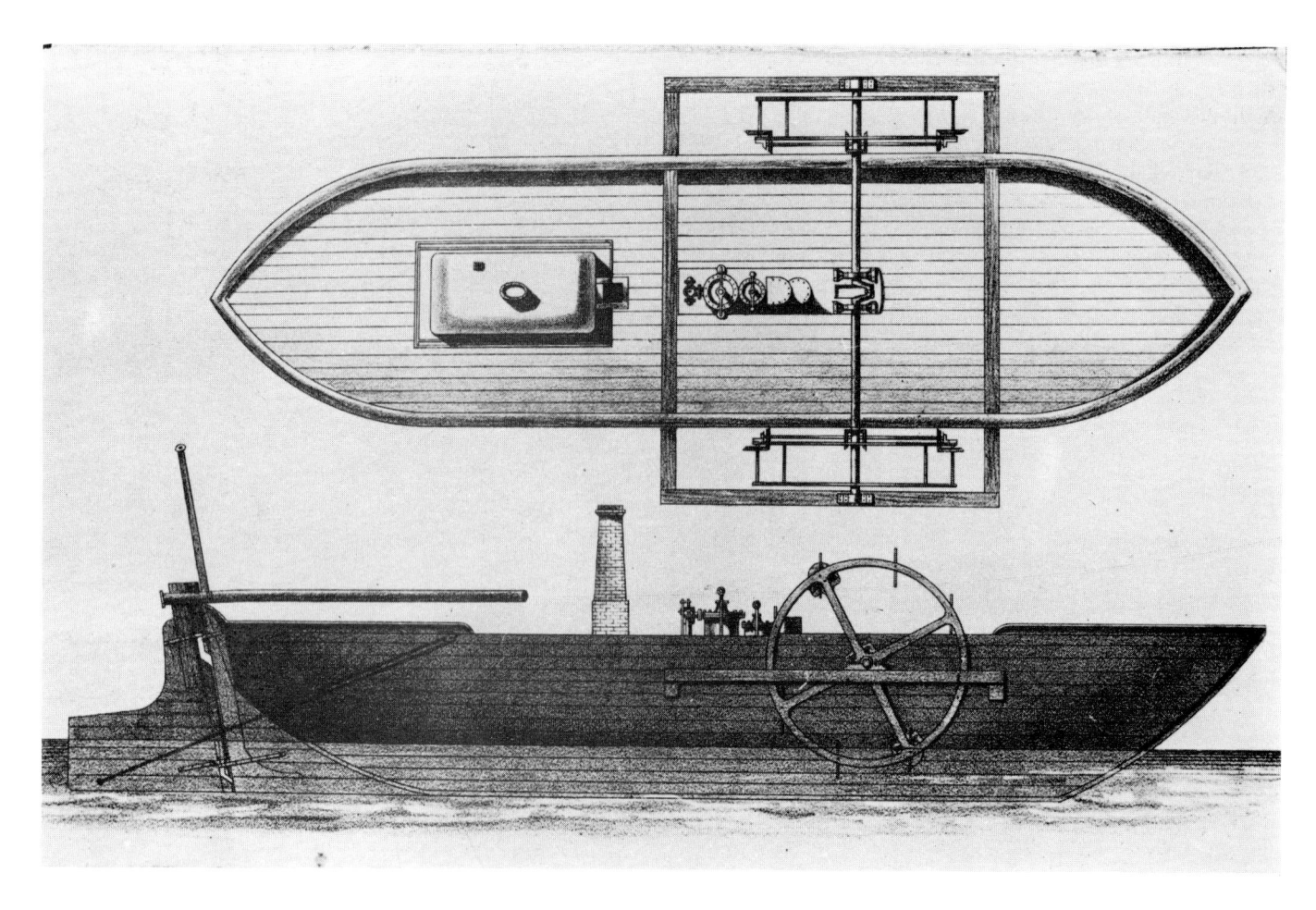

Charles Baird's (and Russia's) first steamship, the *Elizaveta*.

works at Kolpino and in 1805 he became director of the great Aleksandrovskaia manufaktura, or textile mill in St Petersburg. Apart from the production of cannon, Gascoigne was involved in numerous other activities, including the construction of steam engines and mint machinery and the production of buttons.

His achievements were given due acknowledgement by the three Russian rulers whom he served. By 1789 he was a knight of the orders of St Vladimir and of St Anna. By 1798 he had risen to the rank of Actual State Counsellor and owned over 2,000 serfs, given to him by the Emperor Paul. He died in August 1806. Not least among his services to Russia had been his bringing talented workmen from Scotland, several of whom went on to achieve eminence and success. Mention might be made of just one.

Charles Baird (d. 1843) worked with Gascoigne for some four years before joining forces in 1792 with the English instrument-maker Francis Morgan (whose daughter he married two years later). Their iron foundry, which ultimately became the biggest in Russia, began operations in 1800. But Baird was an entrepreneur of enormous energy and ambition and he was responsible for building saw- and flour-mills, dock-yards and bridges. But perhaps his most lucrative venture was in the construction of steamships operating on the Neva between St Petersburg and Kronshtadt. In 1815 his first steamship, the *Elizaveta*, made its maiden voyage. In 1817 Baird secured the monopoly he sought; he was granted 'the exclusive use of this right on the rivers and seas of European Russia' for a period of ten years. This meant that Baird not only operated a passenger service but also was responsible for the far more rewarding freight traffic. By 1820 twenty of Baird's steamers were operating on the rivers of Russia and by 1842 no less than ten on the Kronshtadt-St Petersburg route alone.

Portrait of Charles Cameron (second from left) and friends.

III

Exactly twenty years ago, in August/September 1967, Edinburgh provided the first venue for an exhibition of architectural drawings and photographs, illustrating the work of a man who has been called 'Russia's most famous Scot'. Despite elaborating for his patron Catherine a romanticized biography which traced his descent from Jenny Campbell and Cameron of Lochiel, Charles Cameron was a London Scot, the son of a speculative builder. Nevertheless, it was Cameron's ability to produce work in accord with her enthusiasm for the 'Graeco-Roman' rather than his genealogy that impressed the Empress: within months of Cameron's arrival in Russia in 1779 she was writing that 'nous façonnons avec lui ici un jardin en terrace avec bains dessous, galleries dessus', reflecting her interest in his book *The Baths of the Romans* (1772), and anticipating by several years the actual beginning of what was to be his most famous structure. Cameron's first task was, however, to transform rooms within Rastrelli's great baroque palace at Tsarskoe Selo, some fourteen miles from St Petersburg, into more intimate and appealing accommodation. After the successful completion of a suite of eight rooms, known as the First Apartment, he was put to work on two further suites at the south end of the palace. The Fourth Apartment comprised the official reception rooms, where Cameron's versatility in adapting styles other than the Graeco-Roman is revealed in the Arabesque Room, the Lyons Drawing Room and the Chinese Hall; the Fifth Apartment, a suite of six small rooms, was for the Empress's private use and included a bedroom decorated with twenty-two Wedgwood plaques. It was from the Mirror Room of the Fifth Apartment that a door was to open at first-floor level onto the hanging garden that led to the Agate Pavilion and the Colonnade, as the Cameron Gallery was originally known.

Work on the new wing which overlooked the lake in the English park was completed by 1787. Cameron showed his ability to bring the traditional Russian love of the bathhouse and his expert knowledge of the Roman thermae to a happy creative fusion in the bath complex beneath the Agate Pavilion. The first floor presented in its several rooms (Vestibule, Great Hall, Oval Room, Jasper Study and Agate Room) dazzling variations of the natural stone Russia provided in abundance—coloured marbles, malachite, agate, jasper, lapis lazuli, porphiry. The complement to the Agate Pavilion was the Colonnade or Gallery which so delighted Catherine. A long gallery with a roof supported by Ionic columns, it was open on both sides but contained a glazed central area, where the Empress could sit or entertain in cold or inclement weather; it ended in a portico, from which descended two graceful staircases, merging into one at the halfway stage. In 1792, when Catherine was no longer able to negotiate the steep stairs, Cameron built at right angles to the gallery a *pente douce* (*pandus* in Russian), allowing a more gradual access to the park.

Demanding though the work at Tsarskoe Selo proved, Cameron was given other commissions during the same period. Catherine entrusted him with designing a palace for her son Paul and his second wife, the Grand Duchess Mariia Fedorovna, at Pavlovsk, an estate near to Tsarskoe Selo, and also with the planning and landscaping of a garden amidst the thick woodland on the steep banks of the River Slavianka. Near the palace he began in 1780, Cameron laid out formal areas but also designed other areas of the park in the English landscape style, building a number of pavilions and monuments: his Temple to Friendship in the Slavianka valley was the first building he designed in Russia. In both park and palace there was a sense of classical elegance and reserve, and it was to the beloved model of the Palladian villa that Cameron turned in designing a central three-storeyed building surmounted by a shallow dome on a column-encircled drum, which was flanked by two curving single-storeyed colonnaded galleries. In the palace's interiors created by Cameron the classical Roman influences were paramount, but put to an infinitely more intimate application than under his successor Brenna, who replaced him in 1787, when only five of the rooms on the grand floor had been completed.

The third of the great projects in which Cameron was involved in the early 1780s is the least known. Today only the unrestored Cathedral of St Sophia on the edge of the park of Tsarskoe Selo serves as a reminder of the town of Sophia itself. Begun in 1782 and consecrated only in 1788, the modest but impressive Palladian church stood in a wide square surrounded by other stone buildings designed by Cameron. Cameron was responsible for the complete planning of what was to be a model town, incorporated within the general design of the Tsarskoe Selo park and orientated on the Cameron Gallery, from which it could be viewed. Sophia, however, was to exist for a mere thirty years, for in 1808 Alexander I ordered the town to be razed to the ground. Among the buildings to disappear was a street of small wooden houses on stone foundations, known as the 'English Line', in the south-western corner of Sophia. It was here that the workmen whom Cameron recruited in Scotland in 1784 lived.

The details and significance of this curious episode in Scoto-Russian relations have not hitherto been investigated, although Tamara Talbot-Rice provided some information in the Cameron catalogue. She quotes, for instance, the advertisement in the *Edinburgh Evening Courant* of 21 January 1784, which called for masons, smiths, bricklayers and plasterers to work 'for her Majesty the Empress of all the Russias'. For Cameron, unable to communicate with his Russian workers other than through an interpreter and unconvinced of their ability to carry out his projects as he would wish, the response from the Scottish workmen would have been highly gratifying. No less than seventy-three craftsmen signed three-year contracts. They included four master masons, two of whom had particular skills in vault construction, three master bricklayers, two master plasterers and a master smith, backed up by teams of twenty-seven masons, sixteen bricklayers, fifteen plasterers and five smiths. The group of one hundred and forty workmen, wives and children left Scotland on 3 May 1784 and by the middle of June they were installed at Sophia.

The Cathedral of Sophia.

For her Majesty the Empress of all the Russias.

WANTED,

TWO CLERKS, who have been employed by an Architect or very considerable Builder, who can draw well, such as figures and ornaments for rooms, &c. &c.

 Two Master Masons,

 Two Master Bricklayers,

 A Master Smith, who can make locks, hinges, &c.

 Several Journeymen Plasterers,

 Several Journeymen Bricklayers.

It is expected that none will apply who are not fully masters of the above work, and who cannot bring with them proper certificates of their abilities and good behaviour.

The master masons, bricklayers, and smith, must have been employed as foresmen in their different lines. The master bricklayers and men will have a piece of ground given them. As the encouragement to each will be considerable, the best of tradesmen will be expected.

For further particulars apply to Messrs Peter and Francis Forrester and Company, Leith, who will have a good vessel ready to carry them out by the 1st of April next, provided the Baltic is by that time open.

Cameron's advertisement in the *Edinburgh Evening Courant*.

Things did not go as smoothly in Russia as the workmen may have hoped. They did not always see eye to eye with Cameron and they lodged a series of complaints about their working conditions and non-payment of wages according to contract. For their part the Russian authorities did not always appreciate the Scots' methods and habits. In August 1785, the Empress indeed issued an ukaz, one point of which reads as follows:

Insofar as it has been noted that the English workmen arrive late for work and depart early and moreover celebrate not only their own but also our festivals, which causes great delays in the work, it is required that they arrive at work at 6 am during spring and summer and finish at 9 pm on the longest days and at 7 pm on the shortest, with two hours allowed for meals, and moreover, are to celebrate only the festivals of their own faith and Sundays.

By the summer of 1786 four men had been dismissed (Cameron, incidentally, had recommended more), one had absconded back to Scotland and one had died. The remaining men re-negotiated contracts for a further three years, generally seeking improved pay and also asking for their own pastor and teacher (requests that were not granted). In 1790 most of the workmen returned to Scotland, when their work at Tsarskoe Selo was essentially at an end. They had worked principally on the Cold Bath complex and on the Cameron Gallery, but they were also employed on the Chinese Village and on the Grand Orangery as well as on certain buildings in Sophia itself. There is no evidence that any worked at Pavlovsk, but two masons worked at Peterhof at the lapidary works, where stone was prepared for the Agate Pavilion and other rooms.

By the summer of 1790 the weird and wonderful Russian episode in the lives of the majority of the Scottish workmen came to an end and they were to return to Scotland, undoubtedly glad to see their homeland again but without any hopes of a bright future. In Sophia they had lived as a tightly-knit community, largely isolated from Russian life. Over the years there had been some marriages, mainly among their own but also with members of the St Petersburg British community, some births and a few deaths, principally of infants. The one glimpse into their non-working life is provided by documents in the archive of the Grand Lodge of Scotland which reveals that over forty of the workmen successfully petitioned for a charter of erection of a lodge, which was called the Imperial Scottish Lodge of St Petersburg and entered as Lodge No. 207 in the Grand Lodge's roll. This lodge was unique in Russia in that it was composed of operative as opposed to symbolic masons, but nothing is known of its activities.

But not all the workmen returned. Perhaps as many as twenty decided to remain, convinced that their lives and, possibly, their fortunes were now forever linked with Russia. A few, indeed, were to achieve quite remarkable success and eminence.

Adam Menelaws (1749-1831) came to Russia as an experienced master stonemason. He was, in fact, never to work for Cameron at Tsarskoe Selo but because of his particular expertise in the construction of arches and vaulting, he was immediately set to work for the Russian architect Nikolai L'vov on the St Joseph Cathedral in Mogilev, which had been commissioned by Catherine the Great to mark her meeting there with the Emperor Joseph II of Austria. Menelaws worked on the cathedral for over a decade, but not exclusively, for in 1790 he was involved with the Cathedral of Boris and Gleb, also designed by L'vov, at Torzhok. Although in 1800 he was already described as 'un architecte attaché à notre cour', little is known about his work during the reign of Paul I. It is possible that he was working on estates near Moscow, including Count Razumovskii's Gorenki. Between 1801 and 1803 he was again working for Razumovskii on a great mansion set in a large park descending to the Iauza River in the old Foreigners' Quarter of Moscow. It was in Moscow, following the great fire of 1812, that he rebuilt the house on Gor'kii Street which was to become the Moscow English Club (from 1831) and which today houses the Museum of the Revolution. Menelaws' work in Moscow was in the strict classical idiom practised by his patron L'vov; in the last phase of his career, commencing about 1817, when he began to work at Tsarskoe Selo for the first time, he was to reveal greater variety and versatility. Menelaws was

Portrait of Adam Menelaws by Vladimir Borovikovskii.

The Gothic 'cottage' designed by Adam Menelaws at Peterhof.

responsible for a number of buildings and structures mainly in the Alexander Park or 'New Garden' to the west of Giacomo Quarenghi's Alexander Palace, including the White Tower, the Farm, the Llama House and the Arsenal. Most of these were in the newly fashionable Gothic style, as was a 'cottage' that Menelaws built at Peterhof. For Nicholas I Menelaws was also to build, in a quite different style, the great Egyptian Gate with forty-foot piers clad in cast-iron bas-reliefs copied from Egyptian originals.

Menelaws' younger compatriot William Hastie (1755-1832) was a stonemason whose talent was recognized by Catherine who took him into her employ in 1792 on the strength of an album of architectural drawings which he had submitted to her. None of these projects seems to have gone further than the drawing board, but in 1795 Hastie was appointed chief architect to Count Platon Zubov, Governor of the Ekaterinoslav and Taurida regions in Catherine's newly acquired territories in the south of Russia. He worked on the restoration of the Khan's palace at Bakhchisarai and produced another album of drawings of the palace and other monuments of the Crimea. But Hastie's career, like Menelaws's, blossomed in the reign of Alexander I, though in an unexpected way. He was soon to establish a reputation as the foremost designer and builder of cast-iron arched bridges in Russia, beginning with the Politseiskii Bridge over the Moika and followed by a series of other bridges over the canals of St Petersburg. Concurrently, from 1808, Hastie was chief architect at Tsarskoe Selo, which Alexander raised to the status of a regional town. Hastie prepared a new town plan, of which the essential features are retained in the present-day

The Police Bridge over the Moika in St Petersburg, the first in a series of such bridges designed by William Hastie.

town of Pushkin, and one of the houses he built—a two-storeyed wooden house in 1820—still stands and was the home of the poet Anna Akhmatova in the early years of this century. Hastie became one of the most influential town-planners in Russia, overseeing building and re-construction in a score of towns from Siberia to southern Russia, from the north to Belorussia and the Baltic provinces.

Menelaws and Hastie arrived in Russia as bachelors, although both were to marry Scottish girls; in contrast, James Wilson (1749-1821) came with his wife and six children. Wilson, a master smith, gave excellent service to Russia but it was his eldest son Alexander (1776-1866) who achieved lasting fame. The fortunes of the Wilsons were to become linked with those of Charles Gascoigne, for whom they worked at the turn of the century at the Aleksandrovskaia manufaktura in St Petersburg and at the Admiralty's Izhora works at Kolpino. In 1808, Alexander Wilson, still only 32, became director of both works, a position he was to hold until 1856. He became a Russian citizen, rose to be a Major-General of Engineers in 1826 and a Lieutenant-General in 1829.

IV

In the last decades of the 18th century the 'Northern Tour' emerged as a challenging and intriguing variant of the Grand tour for the intrepid British traveller looking beyond the known delights of France, Switzerland and Italy. The numbers of travellers involved and the number of publications to which such travels gave rise are obviously not large compared with figures for other parts of Europe, but they point at least to the growing interest in Scandinavia and Russia in particular.

At various times during Catherine's reign several Scots are found among the greater number of English travellers to Russia. They include both the prominent and the obscure— Patrick Brydone, Lord Selkirk, Lord Hope, Lord Dalkeith (the eldest son of the 3rd Duke of Buccleuch), Sir John Sinclair and Andrew Swinton. In several cases, little is known about their activities or impressions other than in brief mentions in correspondence, but all seem to have been unadventurous in their travels *within* Russia, confining themselves almost exclusively to St Petersburg. Three of them, however, left written accounts of their travels, two of which were published.

The unpublished account proves to be the least interesting, perhaps surprisingly so in view of the literary talents of its author. Patrick Brydone (1736-1818) had won himself a considerable reputation as a travel writer with the publication in 1773 of his *Tour through Sicily and Malta*, on the strength of which he was elected F.R.S. In 1776 he made a round journey from Berlin via Warsaw and Riga to St Petersburg, where he stayed for a month. The notebook he left of his journey records his everyday impressions and activities with no particular order or development. He spent much of his time with members of the sizeable British community in the Russian capital by whom he was generally more impressed than by the sights he saw. Although he shared the general British esteem for Peter the Great, he was inclined to be contemptuous of Russian pretensions to enlightenment, noting that 'since the so much boasted civilization of this nation I have never heard an instance of any Native whose name has been distinguished in the world for any fine art or science'.

A decade after Brydone's visit, St Petersburg was visited by another noted Scot, Sir John Sinclair (1754-1835), who was to achieve fame as the first President of the Board of Agriculture and as an 'improver'. Although in many respects his tour was no different from that of many other visitors, Sir John was an active politician on a rapid, fact-finding mission. In 1780 he had become a Member of Parliament and in 1786 he systematically planned a tour of the northern capitals of Europe, which would fit into the seven-month Parliamentary recess between June 1786 and January 1787. He left London on 29 May, went by ship to Gothenburg and from there to Copenhagen and Stockholm and arrived in Riga on 1 August. He was in St Petersburg for a month, spent a few days in Moscow and travelled south to Kiev, where he arrived on 23 September. On his return to England he prepared his *General Observations Regarding the Present State of the Russian Empire*, which was privately printed in 1787 for distribution among friends and people of influence. His little book is divided into ten sections, opening with a discussion of 'the character and manner of the Russians' but largely concerned with political matters, questions of territorial expansion, and assessments of prominent individuals. Sinclair's obvious intention was to provide a political assessment of the country and the people in power and to advocate to Pitt a programme of future British policy and strategy. His reaction to Russia and the Russians is very negative. He condemns the tyranny of the nobles over their serfs, the excessive luxury in the towns, the general dissipation during the long winters. He believes that 'nothing can be more despotic than the government of Russia' and although he gives a comparatively sympathetic appraisal of Catherine, 'a *hero* in petticoats', he stresses that 'at present she is puffed up beyond all bounds by the success of her reign'. Although Sinclair had arrived with numerous letters of introduction and had been generally well received by the Empress, Prince Potemkin, Princess Dashkova and others, he is consistently scathing about the 'principal personnages' he met. Potemkin, for instance, 'on the whole, with great abilities, is a worthless and dangerous character'.

The tone of Andrew Swinton's *Travels into Norway,*

Denmark, and Russia, in the Years 1788, 1789, 1790, and 1791 (1792) is markedly different from that of Brydone's journal or Sinclair's volume. Structured in the fashionable form of a series of letters to an unnamed friend, *Travels* is the sympathetic response to new places and peoples by a sentimental traveller, anxious to catch atmosphere, ready to delight in the grandeur of buildings and of nature or in the simplicity of folk culture and village life. He is inclined to use 'agreeable' or 'pleasant' or 'touching' rather than words of condemnation or rebuke; at worst, he is 'melancholy', although this state brings its own delights. Little is known about Swinton, other than what he himself conveys in his book. He was, it seems, a kinsman of Admiral Greig, possibly one of the Swintons from around Crail in Fife. He arrived in Russia just after Greig's death and some of the most interesting pages in his book are about Greig's exploits, his family and other British officers in Russian service.

Although, strictly speaking, not the product of a traveller, *Anecdotes of the Russian Empire. In a series of letters, written a few years ago, from St Petersburg* (1784) belongs to the travel genre and is without doubt the most attractive, profound and enduring work on Russia written by a Scot during the reign of Catherine. Its author was William Richardson (1743-1814), a graduate of Glasgow University to which he was to return in 1773 as Professor of Humanity. In 1768 Richardson went to St Petersburg as tutor to the two sons of Charles, Lord Cathcart, who had been appointed British Ambassador Extraordinary. Apparently genuine letters which he had written to correspondents during the four years he spent in Russia were revised by Richardson for publication. He sought to keep 'everything respecting himself as much out of view as possible', but also admitted that there was much in his book that was scarcely relevant to Russia. Although occasionally in his manner and themes and poetic effusions he anticipates Swinton's work, Richardson was more interested in, and better equipped to understand, basic problems of Russian life and society. While not aspiring to write 'a complete Account of the Russian Empire', Richardson provided keener insights into the nature of despotic rule, the relationship of the estates and

Andrew Swinton's sketch of the 'Bronze Horseman', the equestrian statue of Peter the Great in St Petersburg.

national characteristics than are suggested by the title of 'anecdotes'.

It was only in 1796 in a Moscow journal that the first impressions of a visit to Scotland by a Russian were published. This is not to say, however, that the anonymous author, signing himself simply 'a Russian', was the first representative of his nation to venture north of the border. The phenomenon of the Russian Grand Tourist was, nonetheless, characteristic of Catherine's reign, a more or less direct consequence of a decree by her ill-fated husband which freed the gentry from obligatory state service and gave them the opportunity to travel abroad without hindrance. Perhaps as many as a hundred Russian tourists made their way to England in the last decades of the century, particularly in the 1770-80s, but very, very few saw Scotland. But Russians other than tourists were to be found in Scotland; in addition to the students at Scottish universities (discussed in the following section), there was the occasional visitor travelling primarily for reasons other than pleasure.

The most eminent of Russian visitors was Princess Ekaterina Dashkova, sister of the Russian ambassador in London, Count Semen Vorontsov, and a close friend of the Empress (at least in the early years of her reign). The Princess had paid her first visit to England in 1770, when she made a tour to Bath; she returned in 1776, but on this occasion her purpose was to accompany her seventeen-year-old son Pavel to Edinburgh University. The Dashkovs were to stay some two and a half years in Edinburgh and the Prince's academic pursuits there will be described later. However, during the summer vacation of 1777 Dashkova took her son and daughter on a fortnight's tour of the Highlands. Fortunately, a manuscript copy of this tour has been preserved and gives us a glimpse of parts of Scotland which no other Russian visited in the 18th century. The first day, 25 August, took them to the Forth and Clyde Canal and the ironworks at Carron, the destination of other Russians still to be mentioned, but the next day saw them in Perth and already 'Nature begins to change her appearance towards the terrible and the arid', wrote the Princess in one of the few sentences in English in an

Princess Dashkova.

otherwise French text. After visiting the estate of the Duke of Atholl at Dunkeld and waxing lyrical with an appropriate quotation from Pope, she journeyed on to Taymouth Castle, where the aged but active Lord Breadalbane was to be their host for four days, firing off a twenty-four gun salute in their honour and producing a piper, 'habillé et armé, comme l'étaient anciennement les montagnards'. From Taymouth they went across to Inveraray with wretched inns on route, and then through Glencoe to Dumbarton, where her son received the freedom of the town. They arrived back in Edinburgh in September after a tour which left the princess with lasting memories of the beauty of the countryside, of the mountains and lochs, particularly Loch Lomond, but equally with impressions of the poverty and hardship of the lives of many of the inhabitants, of the squalor of some of the inns and of the lack of taste she detected in the buildings of the 'Seigneurs'.

A decade after Dashkova arrived in Edinburgh, a relative, V. N. Zinov'ev, also visited the city as part of an extensive British tour. He remained in Scotland only for a week, dividing his time between Edinburgh and Glasgow and more concerned to meet notable figures and scholars than to describe scenes. He, nevertheless, noted that Edinburgh was 'an old town, very dirty and ugly', although 'they are now building numerous new streets which are very fine'. The 'Russian' whose travel notes were published in 1795, visited only Edinburgh but stayed about four months from November 1790 to February 1791. He was very much the Russian counterpart of Swinton, enthusiastic, sentimental, impressionistic. There is frequently little detail in his effusions, although he is to be credited with the first attempt to describe a kilt in Russian: suggesting that Lowland Scots do not like the Highlanders, he adds that 'these Highlanders of the male sex wear a short coat and small boots without stockings, and instead of underclothes they wear a sort of skirt, which does not quite cover their knees. I won't go into further details and leave the rest to your imagination'. He finds Edinburgh New Town very attractive, although the squares seem too vast; he considers Sundays 'more strictly observed' in Scotland than in England; and he whiled away an agreeable evening, watching Scottish reels and talking with a pretty Scots lass who had lived five years in St Petersburg.

Finally, we find a number of Russians visiting Scotland as part of wider journeys through Britain, visiting factories and canals and meeting industrialists and scientists. The canal engineer Nikolai Korsakov went in 1776 to see Robert Mackell, builder of the Forth and Clyde canal, and then visited the Carron Works, where he was not allowed to see the secret cannon-boring machine or make drawings of other machinery. He remained some three months in Scotland, deeply impressed by the hospitality of the people and the general level of enlightenment. He spent most of his time in Glasgow, where he was apparently made a honorary freeman of the city. Another Russian to be made a freeman of Glasgow was Pavel Demidov (1738-1821), a member of the famous family of Urals ironmasters. Demidov inevitably made his way to Carron, as did Lev Sabakin, the noted self-taught mechanic, in 1786.

V

In 1790 a Russian visitor to Scotland suggested that 'to the extent that London is a merchant's city, so Edinburgh is a scholar's. It has world-famous doctors of medicine and of jurisprudence. All who wish to perfect their knowledge of medicine come here to study'. And during the years 1774 to 1787 the foreign students in Edinburgh included at different times no fewer than fifteen Russians, several of whom studied medicine. But the story of the Russian students at Scottish universities begins just before Catherine came to the throne and in Glasgow, not Edinburgh.

Semen Desnitskii and Ivan Tret'iakov, students of Moscow University, arrived in Glasgow in 1761 and in the course of the next few years pursued the broad range of subjects which qualified them for their Master's degree in 1765 and 1764 respectively. They were fortunate in the teachers they found at that period in Glasgow: they followed lectures on Ethics and Jurisprudence and also on Rhetoric and Belles-Lettres delivered by Adam Smith, the Professor of Moral Philo-

An Extract from the minutes of Comitia of Glasgow University, 6 January 1767, in which the Russian student, Semen Desnitskii, apologises for some misconduct. (By permission of Glasgow University Archives.)

sophy until his retirement in 1764, and on Roman and British Law by Professor James Millar. They attended, apparently with some reluctance, classes on mathematics conducted by Professor James Williamson, but were also present at Professor James Black's lectures on latent heat in the winter of 1764-5. It was Black who, together with the University Principal, William Leechman, supplied Moscow University with testimonials of the students' progress in 1765. Desnitskii and Tret'iakov, determined to continue their studies for doctorates in law, successfully resisted attempts to recall them to Russia. Although Desnitskii endangered his career by becoming involved in an unfortunate and unpleasant incident with the Professor of Moral Philosophy, John Anderson, he and his friend were awarded their degrees of Doctor of Law and returned to Moscow in the early summer of 1767. Both became Professors of Law at Moscow University, but it was the much more talented Desnitskii who was to reveal the originality and brilliance which earned him the title of the 'father of Russian jurisprudence'. But to his development as a scholar his years at Glasgow and, pre-eminently, the teaching of Smith and Millar made a significant contribution.

When Russian students again appeared in Scotland in the following decade, it was to Edinburgh that they made their way. During the 1760s and 1770s the University flourished under the dynamic leadership of William Robertson and attracted a professoriate eclipsing even that of Glasgow of the previous decade and including, indeed, former Glasgow professors in Joseph Black and William Cullen. Interestingly, it was a graduate and former teacher at Glasgow who was instrumental in establishing the first direct Russian links with Edinburgh. John Robison relinquished his post at Glasgow to go to St Petersburg in December 1770 as secretary to Admiral Sir Charles Knowles. After working for Knowles for two years, Robison became Professor of Mathematics at the Naval Cadet Corps in Kronshtadt in the summer of 1772. The following year he was elected to the chair of Natural Philosophy at Edinburgh and on his return to Scotland in 1774 took with him three young cadets to study at the University. Stepan Rachinskii, Nikolai Beliaev and Ivan Shishukov thus became the first Russians to appear on the matriculation rolls of the university. It would appear that over the next three years they took courses with Robison, the Professor of Mathematics Dugald Stewart, and in one instance, with Adam Ferguson, the Professor of Moral Philosophy. It is possible that they returned to Russia on board a Russian warship, that of Admiral Greig, who left Edinburgh on 9 October 1777 after his triumphant visit to his homeland. At all events, Rachinskii was soon to become Greig's adjutant, while Beliaev and Shishukov returned to the Cadet Corps as instructors in French and English respectively. A further instance of their closeness to Greig is that they all became prominent members of the naval masonic lodge 'Neptune', of which the Admiral was the Master.

During their stay in Edinburgh the three cadets had been joined by another Russian student, none other than Prince Pavel Dashkov, the son of the renowned Princess Dashkova. Princess Dashkova knew precisely what she wanted her son to do, planning not only the courses he was to take but also leisure activities. A fellow student noted that 'Prince Dashkov attends his classes with great assiduity and has perfectly melted away all the Russian Boorishness in French courtesy'. By all accounts he was a model student but mere wax in his mother's hands. She kept open house at their home in the New Town for the cream of Edinburgh society but particularly for the university's professors:

I made the acquaintance of the University professors, all of whom were generally esteemed for their intelligence, intellectual distinction and moral qualities. Strangers alike to envy and the pretentiousness of smaller minds, they lived together in brotherly amity, their mutual love and respect making of them a group of educated and intelligent people whom it is always an immense pleasure to see and whose conversation never failed to be instructive.

Prince Dashkov proceeded smoothly to his Master's degree in the spring of 1779. On 7 May he was made a Freeman of Edinburgh and at the beginning of June the Dashkov family left the 'Athens of the North' for the last time, but not before the Princess had made one final gesture of her esteem for the university. She presented a magnificent cabinet containing a complete set of Russian medals from the birth of Peter the Great to that of the future Alexander I in 1777. Professor Robison was charged by the Senate with the preparation of a detailed description, but at his death, some twenty-five years later, only two sheets of paper were found, which seemed 'to be all that he had performed in the Way of a Catalogue'.

Not all Russian students were as dedicated as Dashkov but not all were as irresponsible as Ivan Sheshkovskii, son of the infamous head of Catherine's Secret Chancellery. Sheshkovskii soon neglected his studies (with Robison, Ferguson and Hugh Blair) to idle away his time and indulge in acts of tomfoolery. Dashkova, who had offered him her protection, more or less washed her hands of 'that brainless youth'. Within months of the Dashkovs' departure from Edinburgh, Sheshkovskii earned himself the unenviable distinction of being the first Russian to be confined in Edinburgh's notorious debtors' prison, the Tolbooth, where he languished for a month in what he himself called 'a situation which is like death itself'.

Dashkova's solicitude was obviously better directed towards Evstafii Zverev, who, like so many Russian students in Britain who had been sent by official bodies, suffered endless privations as a result of not receiving money for his maintenance. Zverev, nevertheless, managed to follow courses in the Edinburgh medical school, but the degree of M.D. which he received on 24 May 1779 was awarded by the University of St Andrews. The degree was conferred *gratis* on account of merit and personal circumstances after testimonials had been furnished by two sympathetic doctors. Zverev was a deserving case and he went on to devote the rest of his long life to medical care, principally in southern Russia.

The fame of the Edinburgh medical school attracted other Russians, including two who had already received their M.D. from other foreign universities. Dr Andrei Italinskii, a graduate of Leiden University, studied at Edinburgh in 1774-5, and a decade later he was followed by Dr Martyn Terekhovskii, whose M.D. was from Strasbourg. Terekhovskii stayed for only a few months but was accorded a warm welcome in

Edinburgh medical circles and was soon elected to honorary membership of both the Medical and Natural History Societies. His election to the latter society was no doubt engineered by another Russian, Iurii Bakhmetev, who was at that precise period one of its four annual presidents. Bakhmetev had come to Edinburgh in 1780 and was himself elected to the Medical Society in December 1783 and to the Natural History Society the following year. The records of the latter society preserve two papers which he delivered: the first was entitled 'On the Use & Action of Quicklime & Other Calcareous Earth as a Manure' (31 March 1785) and the second 'On Coal' (15 December 1785). In 1786 Bakhmetev defended his M.D. thesis, *De variolis inserendis*, dedicated by permission to Catherine II, whose own interest in the subject of smallpox inoculation is well-known. St Andrews also awarded Bakhmetev an M.A. in 1786 and he was also elected a Fellow of the Royal College of Physicians. Highly regarded by Joseph Black as 'a young man of abilities & good sense', Bakhmetev seems regrettably not to have pursued a career in medicine on his return to Russia in October 1787.

A final medical student who did put his considerable knowledge and expertise to good use in his homeland was Daniil Pischekov, who enrolled for classes in the Edinburgh school of medicine in 1783. Pischekov had gained some practical medical knowledge in Russia and this enabled him to qualify for his M.D. some two years later. Once again, however, the award was not from Edinburgh but from another Scottish university, this time Aberdeen. It was in Edinburgh, nevertheless, that his thesis, *De novo methodo psoram sanandi*, was published.

Three further Russians, all members of the gentry, are found studying at Edinburgh in the late 1780s. Mention might be made of one of them. Pavel Bakunin, a nephew of the Russian ambassador in London and officially attached to the embassy, spent most of his time in Edinburgh between 1785 and 1787. He was elected to the Natural History Society in April 1786 and in the following year duly read a paper, as required of members, 'On the Means Used by Nature for the Preservation of Vegetables from the Effects of Cold during the Winter in High Latitudes'. He was not concerned to proceed to a degree, but he returned to Russia with a lasting affection for the University and an admiration for one of its professors in particular, to which he was able to give explicit expression a few years later. In 1794 Bakunin became Director of the Academy of Sciences and one of the few things that he managed to do during his short and unhappy period of office was to engineer against considerable opposition the election of Professor Dugald Stewart as an honorary member, in September 1795.

VI

However unfortunate the circumstances surrounding Stewart's election, his recognition was an example of yet another form of link between Scotland and Russia during Catherine's reign. The elections of eminent scholars and outstanding individuals of another nationality or indeed expatriates as corresponding, honorary or foreign members of societies and learned bodies were marks of mutual respect among nations and opened channels for the communication of scientific, literary, archaeological and other information. The Russian Academy of Sciences, for instance, had elected, under different Directors, other Scots besides Stewart. In December 1776 Dr John Rogerson, Catherine's Scottish physician, was elected to honorary membership. Princess Dashkova herself became Director of the Academy a few years after her return from Scotland and was quick to bestow honorary foreign membership on both Robertson and Black, and honorary membership on Admiral Greig. Following Black's death, the Academy elected Robison to succeed him in 1800. For its part, the Royal Society of Edinburgh counted among its founder members in 1783 Rogerson and another expatriate doctor, Matthew Guthrie, one of the most active suppliers of Russian 'intelligence' to Scotland; it was soon to elect the botanist P. S. Pallas of the Academy of Sciences, John Grieve, yet another Scottish doctor in Russian service, and Ivan (not Pavel) Bakunin. Pavel Bakunin was made a corresponding member of the Society of Antiquaries of Scotland, as were Grieve, Guthrie and William Porter, a prominent Scottish merchant in St Petersburg. Guthrie was a member of the Imperial Free Economic Society, to which James Anderson and Sir John Sinclair were elected in 1792 and 1793 respectively.

The conspicuous role played by Scottish doctors in 18th-century Russia, of whom Rogerson, Grieve and Guthrie are but three outstanding examples from the reign of Catherine the Great, has been examined in detail by Dr Appleby in another contribution to this publication and has, therefore, been omitted from my own. Nevertheless, it is relevant to emphasize here their activities in promoting Scoto-Russian contacts not only in the medical field but also in many other areas of cultural concern. Grieve and Guthrie contributed papers to Scottish (and English) scholarly journals, but Guthrie, in particular, reached out to wider audiences. Between 1792 and 1794 he contributed over forty pieces on many aspects of Russian history, literature, folklore, natural history and exploration to the Edinburgh periodical, *The Bee, or Literary Weekly Intelligence*, edited by James Anderson. Rogerson's services, in contrast, were more of the behind-the-scenes variety. It was he who was responsible for bringing William Robertson's *History of the Reign of the Emperor Charles V* to Catherine's attention and for transmitting his request for information about Russian discoveries along the American seaboard in connexion with his work on *The History of America*. Catherine's interest in Robertson's works undoubtedly led to their inclusion among books designated for translation by the Society for the Translation of Foreign Books (1768-83). Volume I of *Charles V* appeared in 1775, translated from the French version, and Volume II three years later, but although a third volume was translated, it was never published. A similar fate befell *The History of America*, of which only the first part appeared, this time translated directly from the English original, in 1784.

Catherine's reign was marked by an unprecedented upsurge in translating and publishing activity. Scottish authors were comparatively well represented. Journals carried numerous translations of parts of James Thomson's *The Seasons*, although it was only in 1798 that a full separate version was published. Three novels by Tobias Smollett appeared in the late 1780s, but credit for their composition was given to Henry Fielding rather than to poor Smollett! Russia, like so many other European countries, was swept with an enthusiasm for the poems of Ossian and versions appeared in journals and, later, in separate editions. In other areas, one might note translations of John Bell's *Travels* in 1776, James Ferguson's *Lectures on Select Subjects in Mechanics...* in 1784, William Buchan's *Domestic Medicine* in 1790, James Boswell's *Account of Corsica* in 1773, William Hamilton's *Account of the Earthquakes in Calabria* in 1783, David Hume's *Essays Moral and Political* in 1779 and John Williams's *Account of Some Remarkable Ancient Ruins, Lately Discovered in the Highlands... of Scotland* in 1797. Apart from Robertson's, works by other Edinburgh professors to appear in Russian translation included Hugh Blair's *Essays on Rhetoric*, John Gregory's *A Father's Legacy to His Daughters*, both in 1791, and Francis Home's *Principia Medicinae* in 1786.

Major works by Scottish professors and by other eminent literati and philosophers which were not translated into Russian at this period, nevertheless, found their way to Russia in the original English or in French or German versions. Adam Smith's *Wealth of Nations* was held in great esteem by the Russian ambassador in London, Semen Vorontsov, who sent a copy of the book to his brother Alexander, in St Petersburg, and by Princess Dashkova. Vorontsov's brother-in-law, V. N. Zinov'ev, records a meeting with Smith in Edinburgh in August 1786 and describes him to Vorontsov as 'the author of that book, admired by both you and me'. Zinov'ev also spoke with James Burnett, Lord Monboddo, author of *Antient Metaphysics* and *Of the Origin and Progress of Language*, copies of which were sent to Catherine. The traffic was not one-way. Robison at Edinburgh and William Richardson at Glasgow were able to provide informed comment on the Russian scene and other Scottish scholars, such as Robertson, Millar and Lord Kames, reveal much interest in Russian historical development and the contemporary scene in their writings.

The last quarter of the 18th century has been termed Scotland's 'age of recognition'. Russia provides ample evidence of the degree to which it recognized the pre-eminence of Scotland in many areas. Scotland for its part manifests its considerable interest in Russia during the same period—as a trading partner, as a place of employment, as a country to visit, as a subject for study.

SUGGESTIONS FOR FURTHER READING

R. P. Bartlett, 'Scottish Cannon Founders and the Russian Navy, 1768-1785', *Oxford Slavonic Papers*, New Series X (1977), pp. 51-72.

R. P. Bartlett, 'Charles Gascoigne in Russia. A Case Study in the Diffusion of British Technology, 1786-1806', in A. G. Cross, ed., *Russia and the West in the Eighteenth Century*, Mass., 1983, pp. 354-63.

A. G. Cross, 'Arcticus and *The Bee* (1790-1794): An Episode in Anglo-Russian Cultural Relations', *Oxford Slavonic Papers*, N. S. II (1969), pp. 62-76.

A. G. Cross, 'Samuel Greig, Catherine the Great's Scottish Admiral', *Mariner's Mirror*, lx (1972), 173-97.

A. G. Cross, 'By the Banks of the Thames': Russians in Eighteenth-Century Britain, Mass., 1980.

A. G. Cross, 'Charles Cameron's Scottish Workmen in Russia', forthcoming in *Scottish Slavonic Review* (1988).

Tamara Korshunova, 'William Hastie in Russia', *Architectural History*, xvii (1974).

D. S. Macmillan, 'The Scottish-Russian Trade: Its Development, Fluctuations, and Difficulties, 1750-1796', *Canadian-American Slavic Studies*, iv (1970), 426-42.

D. S. Macmillan, 'Problems in the Scottish Trade with Russia in the Eighteenth Century: A Study in Mercantile Frustration', in A. G. Cross, ed., *Great Britain and Russia in the Eighteenth Century: Contacts and Comparisons*, Mass., 1979, pp. 164-81.

K. A. Papmehl, 'Matthew Guthrie—the Forgotten Student of Eighteenth Century Russia', *Canadian Slavonic Papers*, xi (1969), pp. 167-82.

H. J. Pitcher, 'A Scottish View of Catherine's Russia: William Richardson's *Anecdotes of the Russian Empire* (1784)', *Forum for Modern Language Studies*, iii (1967), pp. 236-71.

Isobel Rae, *Charles Cameron, Architect to the Court of Russia*, London, 1971.

Franco Venturi, 'From Scotland to Russia: an Eighteenth-Century Debate on Feudalism', in A. G. Gross, ed., *Great Britain and Russia in the Eighteenth Century: Contents and Comparisons*, Mass., 1979, pp. 2-24.

THROUGH THE LOOKING-GLASS: SCOTTISH DOCTORS IN RUSSIA (1704-1854)

JOHN H. APPLEBY

BETWEEN 1704, the year in which Robert Erskine arrived at Moscow, and 1854 when Sir James Wylie died in St Petersburg, there was a 150-year dynasty—a baker's dozen of Scottish doctors who effectively transformed the Russian medical system. Through their writings and general activities they also exercised considerable influence, largely overlooked, upon their contemporaries at home: the medical profession, natural historians, scientists and those engaged in the arts. The aim of the present essay is to highlight their main achievements as succinctly as possible.

At least ten out of these thirteen Scots received their education at the University of Edinburgh. Many factors motivated them to seek employment in Russia: greater scope for practice and preferment; political reasons; family links and recommendations; a thirst for knowledge and experience; or, quite simply, sheer adventurousness.

Robert Erskine, who founded this dynasty, was born in 1677, the sixth surviving son of Sir Charles Erskine of Alva and a cousin of the Earl of Mar. Apprenticed at fifteen to Hugh Paterson, an Edinburgh surgeon-apothecary, he was also inscribed at the university, but without taking a degree. He studied anatomy, surgery, chemistry and botany for two years in Paris before graduating M.D. at Utrecht in 1700. Becoming a skilful dissector and lecturer on anatomy at a London medical school, his reputation ensured his election to the Royal Society in November 1703.

Arrival in Russia: the First Archiater

Probably as a result of Peter the Great's recruitment drive, Robert Erskine went to Moscow in 1704, first as physician to Prince Menshikov, Peter's principal lieutenant, and then, in 1705, as doctor to the Tsar. The following year he was appointed Peter's chief physician and archiater—the first person in Russia to hold both the office and the title. As archiater, or president of the Apothecaries' Chancery (renamed the Medical Chancery in 1725), Erskine occupied the highest position in the Russian medical hierarchy, with overall responsibility for civilian and military medicine, the apothecaries, pharmacy, botanical gardens and so forth. At only 29 years of age, this was a high tribute to his powers of planning and organization. By all accounts Erskine was very successful in reorganizing the Chancery, placing it on a sound financial basis and greatly increasing its efficacy, both at Moscow and later on when it transferred to the new capital at St Petersburg in 1710.

Erskine's own collection of plants growing in and around Moscow, dated 1709, is the earliest surviving Russian herbal. It has been preserved in very good condition at the Botanical Institute of the USSR Academy of Sciences in Leningrad, itself an offshoot from the St Petersburg Apothecaries' Garden, Russia's first specifically physic garden pioneered and superintended by Robert Erskine (or 'Areskine', as he was called by the Russians) from 1714.

In 1713 the Royal Society of London, prompted by political and scientific considerations, formed a 'Committee for Russia'; its sixteen members included Isaac Newton, Edmund Halley, James Petiver and Richard Mead. The list of the 53 enquiries drawn up, covering many fields such as Russian medicine and natural history, was sent to Erskine and

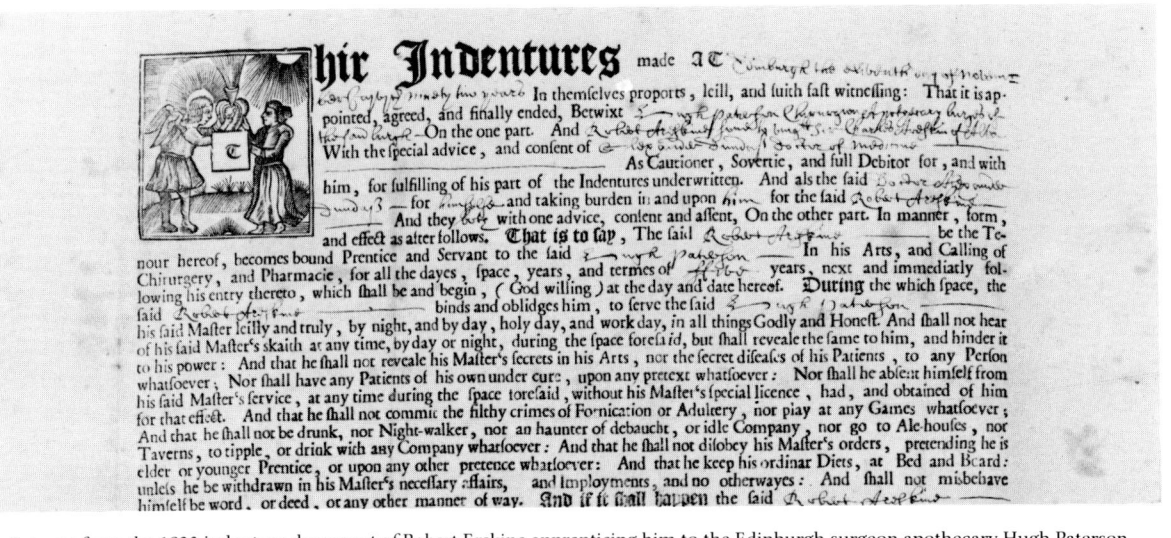

Extracts from the 1692 indenture document of Robert Erskine apprenticing him to the Edinburgh surgeon-apothecary Hugh Paterson.

to Henry Farquharson, professor of mathematics from Aberdeen University, who ran the Tsar's School of Mathematics and Navigation at Moscow until 1715. Whether they replied is not known, but the episode marks a development of interest in the Russian natural scene and had repercussions. Erskine purchased some outstanding natural and medical collections for Russia's first natural history museum (constituting the nucleus of the Academy of Sciences, founded in 1725): the Dutchmen, Albert Seba's and Frederick Ruysch's famous cabinets and anatomical models, Maria Sybille Merian's beautiful watercolours of insects, and several others.

As the Tsar's chief physician, Erskine accompanied him on most of his journeys and numerous military campaigns. Two notebooks he kept of Peter's health survive. One of these provides a detailed medical account of his treatment at Carlsbad spa between 9 and 27 October 1712. The second diary records the monarch's main ailments from 17 February to 18 December 1714, particularly on a journey from St Petersburg to Revel (Tallinn, Estonia). On one occasion the monarch had violent indigestion after washing down oysters with beer—Erskine prescribed a medicine, and the Tsar was able to sleep it off!

When Erskine fell under suspicion of Jacobitism in 1716, Peter the Great, then at the Hague with his physician, strenuously denied all implications in a letter he wrote to the British Secretary of State; and he presented Erskine with an inscribed gold snuff-box, set with agate stones, as a token of his trust. Earlier, at Danzig, the Tsar had issued a special charter, appointing Erskine a councillor of state for his 'numerous and most faithful services', and reconfirming him in his posts.

Robert Erskine died, 41 years old, on St Andrew's Day in 1718. He was given a magnificent funeral by Peter. The monarch acquired his collection of minerals, shells, surgical instruments, medals and Asian curiosities that eventually constituted part of the Academy's Museum in 1726. Erskine's library, one of the best in its day, along with Archibald Pitcairne's, purchased by Erskine for the Tsar, formed a cornerstone of the Library of the Russian Academy of Sciences. Transcripts of their catalogues are in the Department of Manuscripts at the National Library of Scotland.

Thomas Garvine in Chinese costume. (By permission of the Library of the Wellcome Institute.)

Travels and Expeditions

Although Robert Erskine died in 1718, he planned many of the details of Russia's first natural history expeditions—to the Caucasus under Dr Gottlob Schober (1717-20), and to Siberia under Dr Daniel Gottlieb Messerschmidt (1720-27).

One of Erskine's protégés was Thomas Garvine, born at Ayr in 1690. Garvine, apprenticed to John Marshall, a Glasgow surgeon who later became superintendent of the University's physic garden, occupied a surgeon's post at a St Petersburg hospital sometime shortly before 1713. When the third Earl of Loudoun recommended him to Erskine, he was sent on Russia's earliest medical mission to China, between 1715 and 1718. Written and visual evidence indicates that he may have been the first person to introduce the Chinese method of smallpox variolation on his return to Russia. A life-size painting, attributed to William Mosman, portrays Garvine in Chinese costume, pointing to a table on which there is a box of lancets used for inoculations; at the foot of the table is a Latin document about his mission. Garvine returned to Scotland soon afterwards and was elected provost of Ayr on five occasions.

Garvine's neighbour, John Bell of Antermony, in Stirlingshire, studied medicine at Glasgow University before entering the Russian medical service in 1714, equipped with a letter of recommendation to Robert Erskine. Erskine obtained a post for him on a Russian mission to Persia, from 1715 to 1718. Six months after his return (Erskine had died six weeks before), Bell went on another mission, to China, travelling overland through Siberia and Mongolia to Peking, and returning to the Russian capital in January 1722. His book, *Travels from St Petersburg in Russia to Diverse Parts of Asia*, a classic of its kind published in 1763, contains many vivid descriptions of Russian and Chinese natural history. Bell supplied Sir Hans Sloane with numerous objects, particularly a mammoth tusk. Sloane contributed a memoir on the subject to the French Academy's *Histoire* for 1727, while his and several related papers appeared in the Royal Society's *Philosophical Transactions*. One of the more significant of these was by William

Hunter, the famous anatomist. He pointed out, in 1768, that it was not an elephant's tusk, as Sloane had thought, but a mammoth's. A manuscript in John Bell's hand, 'Sundry anecdotes of Peter the First', presents lively thumbnail sketches of the Tsar with whom he obviously enjoyed a good relationship—witness the elegant glass goblet and tumblers inscribed with the imperial arms in gold and Bell's monogram presented to him by the Tsar.

Goblet and glasses presented to John Bell by Peter the Great.

A third Scottish traveller, from the same parts as Bell and Garvine, was John Cook, born at Hamilton in 1712. Trained as a surgeon in London, Cook went to Russia in 1736 on health grounds. After a brief spell at a military graduate hospital, he worked at the St Petersburg General Naval Hospital for a couple of years. Subsequently he was employed as a family doctor to Prince Galitzin in the Azov area, until in 1741 he was appointed chief physician to the port of Astrakhan. At the same time he supervised the construction and running of the Astrakhan Naval Hospital, overseeing the local field regiments and garrison hospitals. He was dismissed from these posts, at his own request, in May 1745, in order to accompany Prince Galitzin on a three-year embassy to the Persian court. Following this, he was promoted surgeon-general to Count Lacy's army at Riga. In 1756 he was made an M.D. of St Andrews University on the basis of testimonials. He returned in 1757 to Hamilton where he practised medicine till his death in 1804.

John Cook's two volumes of *Voyages and Travels through the Russian Empire, Tartary and Part of Persia*, published at Edinburgh in 1770, make excellent reading. Not only do they convey a vigorous impression of his own career and experiences, but they also provide invaluable first-hand accounts of medicine and natural history in Russia during the reigns of Anne and Elizabeth. For instance, they show that Cook performed a significant role in the diagnosis, treatment and prevention of the plague that ravaged the Don region during 1738 and 1739. He describes in detail his practical measures for combating it, which were endorsed and implemented by the Medical Chancery. Considerable space is given to the Russians' treatment of scurvy. Cook expounds his own views about this dreaded disease. His observations on scurvy at Taverhoff, Astrakhan and Riga were incorporated in the form of a letter published in James Lind's celebrated *Treatise on Scurvy* (1753).

Cook's *Voyages* contain much interesting information about natural history. In addition he corresponded from Astrakhan with Peter Collinson, the well-known English naturalist, offering to undertake any commissions for him or other members of the Royal Society. In fact, he supplied the Society with specimens and a great deal of useful knowledge about the Russian natural scene, most of it resulting from his own experiments and observations. This comprises detailed replies to queries about the beluga whale, or sturgeon, and the alleged medical characteristics of the stone found in it; the different kinds of natural salts, such as Persian borax, located around Astrakhan; and the white and black naphtha at the site of today's Baku oilfields.

James Grieve graduated in medicine from Edinburgh University in 1733. After wide experience as a military doctor, he was appointed City Physician to St Petersburg in October 1747. This very responsible position involved working in close contact with the Medical Chancery, supervising apothecaries and medicines, arresting unqualified practitioners, passing forensic judgments, and a host of other duties. A few years later, as stated in his petition for membership of the Royal College of Physicians of Edinburgh (he was elected a fellow in 1753), he became physician to the Empress Elizabeth, returning to Britain in 1757. However, Grieve's chief claim to fame is that he was the first in the West to translate, although in a curtailed version, S. P. Krasheninnikov's pioneering *History of Kamchatka*. Krasheninnikov participated in the Second Kamchatkan, or Great Northern Expedition (1733-50), launched by the Russian Academy under Vitus Bering. He was appointed professor of botany and natural history as a result of his field researches and his book, published in 1759, is the earliest scientific survey of Kamchatka. James Grieve's translation, published in 1765 (the year after he died, at St Petersburg where he may have been physician to Catherine the Great), helped to open Westerners' eyes to the natural riches of the Russian Far East.

With the Russian Army: the Last Archiater

James Mounsey, born at Skipmire, Dumfriesshire, in 1710, received a broad medical education at Edinburgh University. He signed a contract for employment in Russia in 1736 and, after a brief period at the St Petersburg Naval Hospital, enlisted with the army in the Ukraine (Russia was then at war with Turkey). He served under General Münnich on the Dnieper, but left the forces in 1738 to accompany General James Keith, his compatriot, to Paris so that Keith could be treated for a war wound. Mounsey used the opportunity to graduate with an M.D. at Rheims University in 1740. The following year he re-enlisted with the Russian army, this time

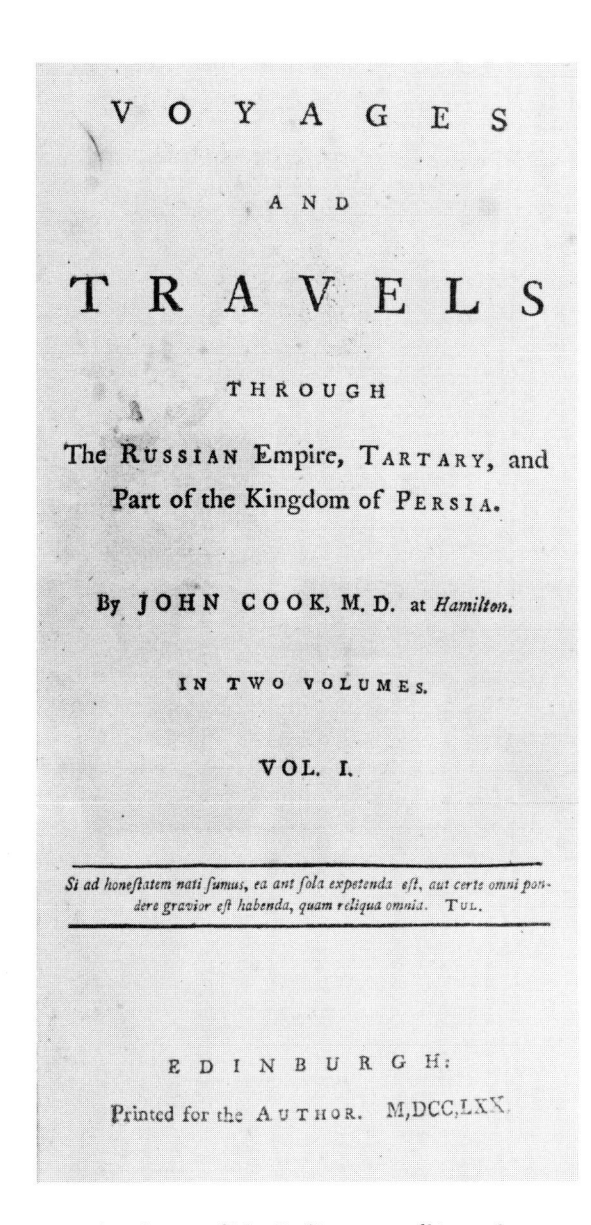

The title-page of John Cook's account of his travels.

James Mounsey, the last archiater of the Russian Medical Chancery.

as a fully qualified physician and surgeon, travelling with it to Finland (during the Russo-Swedish War) and then through Central Europe, obtaining experience and promotion in the Livonian Division, Repnin's Corps and later the First Moscow Division.

It was while Mounsey was with Keith at Åbo in Finland during the Russo-Swedish War that he performed a difficult operation to extract a foetus, lodged in a Finnish woman's fallopian tube for thirteen years. When Henry Baker, the naturalist and secretary to the Royal Society, initiated a correspondence with Mounsey (lasting for 23 years), Mounsey sent an account of this unusual case, and the foetal bones, to the Royal Society who published an abstract of it in the *Philosophical Transactions* for 1748. Over the next few years he dispatched to Baker and the Royal Society large consignments of Russian and Persian minerals, plants, seeds and zoological specimens. All but two of his half a dozen letters to Baker, published in the *Philosophical Transactions*, were written in response to specific requests for details about natural history by members of the Royal Society. Hence, Cook's and Mounsey's accounts and items signify a development of the interest expressed by the Society in its enquiries to Robert Erskine and Henry Farquharson 34 years earlier. Mounsey's papers embraced many topics such as crayfish, castor from beavers, hot springs at Carlsbad, salt mines near Krakow, swallows, earthquakes, poison from the lead in paint, and naphtha. As a result, he was elected a fellow of the Royal Society in March 1750.

Mounsey resigned from the army in 1756, becoming a very successful private practitioner at Moscow, and marrying a relative of James Grieve. In September 1760 he was made the Empress Elizabeth's body physician and given the title of councillor of state. He tended her on her deathbed fifteen months later—his account of her final illness was published in the *St Petersburg Journal*. Elizabeth's successor, Peter III, appointed Mounsey his chief personal physician and archiater, conferring on him the rank of privy councillor. As archiater, Mounsey directed the Medical Chancery. Whereas Erskine had been the first person to occupy this position of supreme authority in the Russian medical hierarchy, Mounsey was the last. Within three months, he had drawn up an excellent table of ranks, integrating military with civilian posts, and issued a detailed precept to doctors about systematizing the dispensing of medicines. They were signed by Peter and ratified as ukazes by the Russian Senate. When the Tsar was murdered on 17 July 1762, Mounsey prudently returned to Scotland and built himself a fine mansion at Rammerscales, near Lochmaben. His part in introducing medicinal rhubarb to Britain is described below (p. 57).

Catherine the Great's Reign (1762-1796)

John Rogerson, born at Lochbrow in the parish of Johnstone (Dumfriesshire) in 1741, represents a fulcrum at the mid-point of the dynasty of Scottish doctors in Russia, with many strands converging on him. His mother was Mounsey's half-sister. Like several other doctors who served in Russia, Rogerson joined the Royal Medical Society of Edinburgh, graduating from the University with an M.D. dedicated to James Mounsey who recommended him for Russian employment in 1766. Three years later he was appointed a court doctor. Rogerson exercised considerable influence over Catherine. For instance, he brought William Robertson's historical works to her notice and conveyed journals and a naval chart of the Russian discoveries which the historian incorporated, with acknowledgments to Rogerson, in his *History of America*. For these and other services Rogerson became the first Briton to be elected to the Russian Academy of Sciences—in 1776. That year the empress made him her personal physician, at some stage presenting him with a set of porcelain medal casts of all her predecessors.

In May 1779 Rogerson was elected a fellow of the Royal Society of London for his 'proficiency in several branches of natural knowledge' and the potential usefulness of his position in Russia. Three of his letters to John Clerk of Eldin, near Edinburgh, endorse his interest in natural history. From the first two, written at St Petersburg in 1772 and 1773, it transpires that Rogerson sent his correspondent parcels of seeds from

John Rogerson, personal physician to Catherine the Great.

larch, pine, cedar, barley and buckwheat gathered from all over Russia, together with some Ukrainian seeds for John Hope, superintendent of the Royal Botanic Garden at Edinburgh, to cultivate. Hope had an account with Rogerson at St Petersburg for these items. Rogerson's third letter to Clerk, dated about May 1783, is even more revealing. It shows that in the autumn of 1782 he had sent John Walker, Regius Professor of Natural History at Edinburgh University, 'at his requisition', over 100 Russian and Siberian minerals, mostly supplied by the famous naturalist Pallas, 'Professor in our Academy and a Man of first rate merit and knowledge'. Rogerson, a consummate diplomatist, also proposed a correspondence between Pallas and Walker, though nothing appears to have come of it. Around this time Catherine commissioned Pallas to compile the *Flora Rossica*, a sumptuous botanical work on 'useful' Russian plants. The first two parts of volume one were printed at St Petersburg in 1784 and 1788/9, respectively. Rogerson circulated copies, either by post or personally, to the Royal Colleges of Physicians of Edinburgh and London, as well as to the Royal Society of London, contacting William Cullen in

August 1785, immediately prior to a visit, to assure him of a copy of the second part.

Rogerson had dealings with most British doctors in Russia during his 50 years' service there (until 1816). One of them, with whom he was on very friendly terms, was Jonathan Rogers, medically trained in London under John Hunter and George Fordyce. He held a post at St George's Hospital for several years, leaving for employment with the Russian navy in 1774, followed by an embassy to Constantinople, several years in the army, five years back in London, and then fifteen years in private Russian medical practice (he was doctor to 149 households!). He returned to Britain from 1799 until 1803 when appointed senior doctor and, in 1804, Physician-General to the Russian fleet. His *Pharmacopoea navalis Rossica* was printed in 1806. It is touching that Jonathan Rogers should have presented his friend, John Rogerson, with two beautifully executed booklets eighteen days before he died (23 May 1811).

John Grieve, related to James who translated Krasheninnikov's book on Kamchatka, was born at Edinburgh in 1753. During his studies at the University he became president of the Physico-Surgical Society graduating, however, M.A. and M.D. at Glasgow University in October 1777. Like his relative, he joined the Russian army, in 1778, recommended by Rogerson, serving with the Voronezh Division until 1783 when he returned to Britain for health reasons. He drew on his experience in Russia to write an account of his treatment of a Russian woman for obstinate dropsy that appeared in Andrew Duncan's *Medical Commentaries*. For the next 15 years Grieve practised medicine as a fashionable London doctor. A great socializer, he was elected to numerous scientific and cultural societies, among them the Societies of Antiquaries of Scotland and London, the Royal Society of Arts, the Bath Agricultural and Philosophical Societies, the Physical Society at Guy's Hospital, the Society for Promoting Natural History, the Society for the Relief of the Widows and Orphans of Medical Men, and the Royal Society of London (May 1794). In 1798 he returned to Russia as court physician, first to Paul and then to Alexander, dying suddenly, at only 52 years of age, in December 1805.

One of the most interesting features of John Grieve's life was his correspondence with Joseph Black, Professor of Medicine and Chemistry at Edinburgh. Grieve had studied under him, and he called on him when he returned from Russia in 1783 (Black and William Robertson were elected foreign members of the Imperial Academy of Sciences on 28 January 1783). Black provided him with an introduction to Jean-Joseph Suë, a distinguished professor of anatomy in Paris. From there, and from the home of Baron Dimsdale who had inoculated Catherine for smallpox, Grieve penned letters to Black, reporting the latest scientific and technical developments in France, such as air-ballooning and his own attendance at Mesmer's demonstration of animal magnetism.

However, it was Grieve's letters to Joseph Black on the subject of kumis, or fermented mare's milk, that have a more direct bearing on Russia. On the strength of a paper by Grieve about kumis, Black engineered his election to the Royal Society of Edinburgh in January 1784—at the same time as Pallas. Grieve's paper, which Black read to the Society, appeared in its first, belated volume of *Transactions* of 1788 under the title, 'An account of the method of making a wine, called by the Tartars koumiss; with observations on its use in medicine'. In it, he explains that when he first thought of its possible medical applications, kumis was as little known in Russia as in Britain. After a detailed description of the Tartar methods and the chemical processes involved in fermenting the substance, he outlines its mode of operation and gives comprehensive case histories of four Russian patients whom he had successfully treated for debility, consumption, digestive disorders, and various nervous illnesses. This pioneering publication created considerable interest at the time, but was then virtually forgotten until 1881 when George Carrick, physician to the British embassy at St Petersburg, and formerly at the Brompton Hospital for Consumption and Disorders of the Chest, wrote a book about kumis, praising John Grieve for being the first to discover and use it in medicine, and to publicize its virtues. Modern research and practice in the Soviet Union confirm many of Grieve's findings of the therapeutic value of kumis.

Matthew Guthrie, born in 1743 and descended from Sir James Guthrie, Royal Falconer in Fife, was apprenticed to an Edinburgh surgeon attached to the Royal Infirmary, and attended medical lectures at the university between 1761 and 1765. The influential Rogerson probably secured his post with the Russian army in which he saw service from 1769 to 1778, when appointed chief physician to the Imperial Land Cadet Corps of Nobles at St Petersburg. He held this position until his death in 1807. A prolific writer, and corresponding or full member of numerous British societies, Guthrie communicated wide-ranging information about Russian medical, natural and cultural history. Many of his letters and papers were published in Andrew Duncan's *Medical Commentaries*, James Anderson's journal, *The Bee* (under the pseudonym of 'Arcticus'), as well as the *Philosophical Transactions* and the *Transactions* of the Royal Society of Edinburgh. His correspondents included eminent scientists such as Joseph Priestley, Joseph Black, Sir Joseph Banks and John Howard, the philanthropist.

In 1778-9 Guthrie wrote three letters to Priestley, explaining how Russian peasants managed to avoid scurvy by their diet and life style, and their method of treating people overcome by fumes from their stoves. John Howard, visiting Russian hospitals and prisons in the summer of 1781, met Matthew Guthrie who wrote for him a very detailed account of the physical education of the remarkably healthy girls at the Imperial Convent of Noble Ladies in St Petersburg, which Guthrie's wife, Maria, had directed. He was elected to the fellowship of the Royal Society in April 1782 for his 'several valuable communications'. Between 1783 and 1786 he wrote several letters to Joseph Black on the subject of experiments to freeze mercury, the conversion of iron into steel, and the famous Bestuzhev Drops used by the Russians as a tonic in the treatment of hysteria and nervous illnesses. Finally, Guthrie contributed a wealth of material to Andrew Duncan's *Medical Commentaries*, renamed *Annals of Medicine* in 1795-6, throughout most of its existence.

Matthew Guthrie was also well versed in the arts. He wrote two letters to the Royal Society of Arts, of which he was a

The first page of John Grieve's article on the therapeutic value of fermented mare's milk.

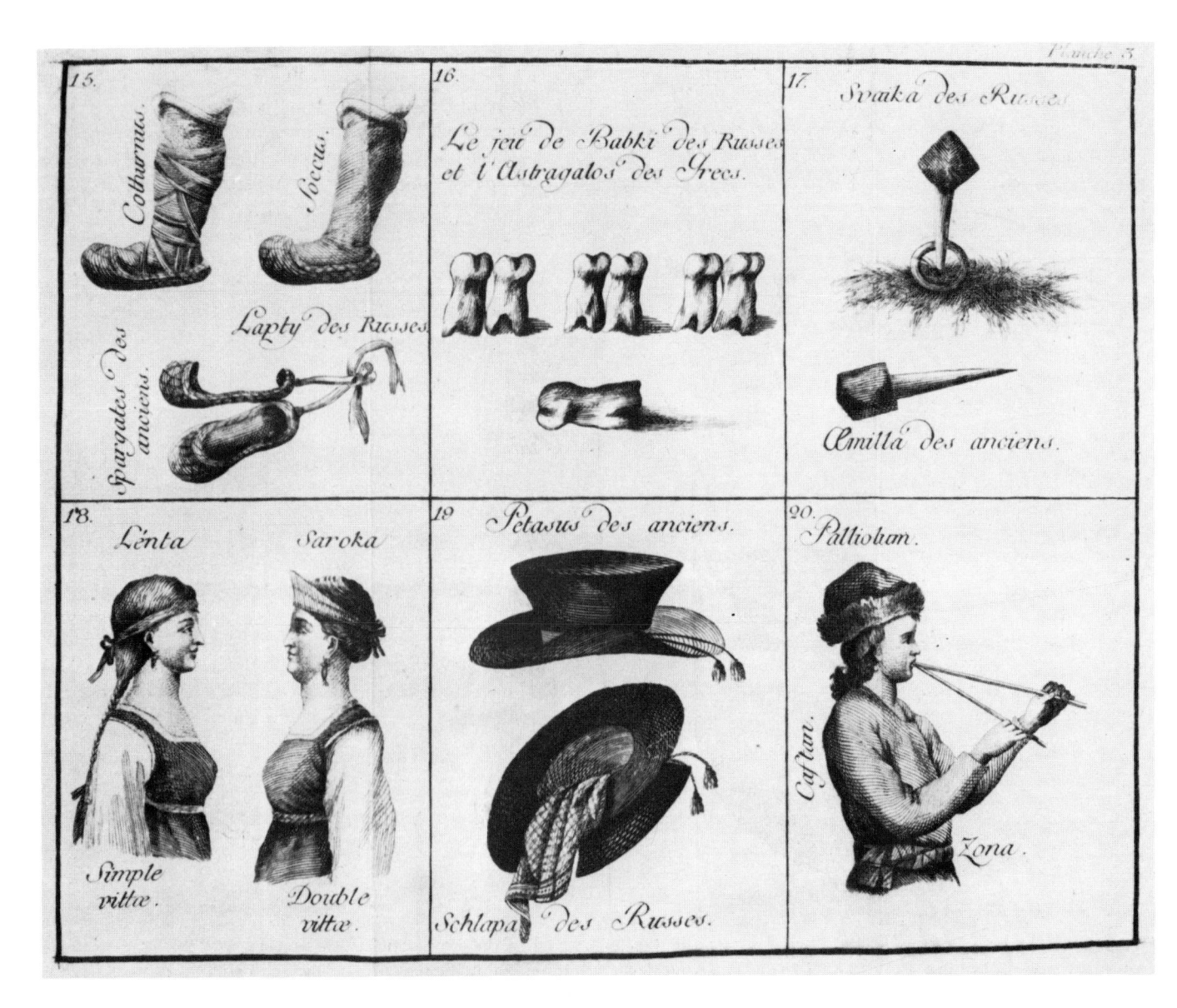

Illustrations of Russian amusements and costume from Matthew Guthrie's 'Dissertations sur les antiquités de Russie'.

corresponding member. With his second letter, dated October 1793, he enclosed samples of the shot hemp manufactured by a secret process in Silesia and sent to Catherine, dyed in different colours. Guthrie's first completed work, *Dissertations sur les Antiquités de Russie*, printed at St Petersburg in 1795, was dedicated both to Catherine and to the Society of Antiquaries of Scotland. It is a remarkable piece of writing which aims to draw parallels between Greek, Scythian and Russian folk music, songs and dancing. Guthrie had been elected a corresponding member of the Antiquaries in 1782 when he presented the Society with a series of 63 Russian medals (dispersed at the end of the 19th century) depicting battles, victories and other events. In 1802 he edited and published, under his wife's name, *A Tour Performed in the Years 1795-6 Through the Taurida, or Crimea*, compiled in the form of cultured, entertaining letters which Maria Guthrie wrote while travelling in southern Russia, collecting information about the parts she visited for her husband.

Two monographs of much interest by Guthrie were intended as additions for a second edition of Maria Guthrie's *Tour*. The first, 'A Supplementary Tour Through the Countries on the Black Sea', is interleaved with copious notes about a wide spectrum of subjects. The second, a companion volume, is entitled a 'Natural History of the Taurida....' Also interleaved, it is a mine of information about all aspects of Crimean natural history, materia medica, and much else besides. Both manuscripts are in the British Library.

Matthew Guthrie was a formidable mineralogist. In October 1786, his letter to James Hutton, the geologist, thanking him for a box of minerals (which he promised to reciprocate with Russian ones) and a copy of his 'little publication', proved that a preliminary account of Hutton's epoch-making *Theory of the Earth* was in print two to three years earlier than previously thought. At the same time, Guthrie complained that the Royal Society of Edinburgh had failed to publish any papers (Guthrie was a member of its forerunner, the Philosophical Society of Edinburgh). In fact, there was a long delay and the Society's first volume of *Transactions* was not published till 1788. Guthrie contributed an intriguing 'Dissertation on the Climate of Russia' to the second volume, printed in 1790.

Between January 1785 and June 1801, Guthrie wrote eight letters to Sir Joseph Banks, president of the Royal Society of London, about Russian minerals, sending him several specimens of new discoveries from Siberia and the Sea of Okhotsk shoreline. Much of the correspondence is taken up with steps to retrieve a large plate of malachite (70x43x5 cm, and requiring two men to lift it), which Matthew Guthrie had sent as a present to King George III in October 1784. The Secretary of State failing to acknowledge the gift after four months, Banks had rescued and kept it for Guthrie. After abortive attempts to sell the malachite for 1,000 guineas and a mishap when Banks nearly broke his leg in an effort to prevent the slab from falling, Guthrie's wife made arrangements for its return to Russia and it was eventually sold to Count Strogonov.

The last letter Guthrie wrote to Sir Joseph Banks in 1801 informed the president that because he had been the principal collector of gemstones in St Petersburg for many years, he had devised and sent a system of classifying them to Dr James Anderson in February 1792 for publication in *The Bee*. As 'Arcticus,' Matthew Guthrie wrote an incredibly wide range of material for this journal from 1792 to 1794: besides his classification of gems, there are articles and anecdotes about Peter the Great, literary topics, the arts, natural history of all kinds, the Russian climate, voyages of discovery, potted biographies, and humorous sketches.

Medicinal Plants from Russia to Scotland

Three important medicinal plants were introduced by Scottish doctors to Britain for the first time: rhubarb (*Rheum palmatum* L.), Siberian snowrose (*Rhododendron aureum* Georgi), and assafoetida (*Ferula persica* Willdenow).

In January 1770 James Mounsey was awarded the gold medal of the Royal Society of Arts for introducing to Britain the seed of medicinal rhubarb that he had sent to Henry Baker from Russia in 1761. Sir Alexander Dick, then president of the Royal College of Physicians of Edinburgh, had corresponded

A drawing of the medicinal rhubarb plant, seeds of which Mounsey had sent to Professor John Hope at the Royal Botanic Garden, Edinburgh.

with Mounsey about the 'true Rhubarb'. When Mounsey returned to Scotland in 1762 he brought a large parcel of the seed, part of which he gave to Dick and part to John Hope, Professor of Botany and Superintendent of the Royal Botanic Garden. For this service Mounsey was elected an honorary fellow of the College in November 1762. Hope, at its request, cultivated the plant successfully, transmitting some seed to the Royal Botanical Garden at Kew and to various patrons or honorary members of the College. He corresponded in 1765 with both Mounsey and John Bell about three different varieties of rhubarb found in Russia and China. His letter to Sir John Pringle about the *Rheum palmatum*, accompanied by a botanical description and drawings of the plant, was published in the *Philosophical Transactions* for 1766. For several decades the Royal Infirmary in Edinburgh used no other root for their medicine.

In 1777 Matthew Guthrie sent Andrew Duncan, Professor of Medicine at Edinburgh University, a small bag of the dried plant from the *Rhododendron chrysanthum* or Siberian snowrose, as it was then called, known technically today as *Rhododendron aureum* Georgi. This shrub was encountered by the naturalist Pallas during his travels through the mountains on the River Enisei. Guthrie's letter, which Duncan printed in his *Medical and Philosophical Commentaries*, inviting his friend to 'try its effects in your part of the world', gives an entertaining account of the plant medicine's intoxicating effects when taken by Siberians for arthritis, rheumatism and gout. Although Duncan did not publicize any experiments which he may have carried out at his Edinburgh Dispensary opened in 1776, he passed on some of the plant to Francis Home, Professor of Materia Medica at the University. Home conducted clinical trials, praising it in his *Chemical Experiments* as 'one of the most powerful sedatives which we have'. Consequently it was introduced into the *Edinburgh Pharmacopoeia*. Modern Russian medicine prescribes it for cardiac insufficiency, as it has an effect on the heart similar to digitalis preparations.

Also in 1777, Guthrie wrote a letter to John Hope, conveyed, along with two assafoetida plants, by James, Lord Hope (later Earl of Hopetoun), returning from St Petersburg where Catherine had received him and his wife very favourably. The letter itself provides significant evidence of a two-way exchange of natural history items (between Pallas and John Hope). It also sheds light on Matthew Guthrie's correspondence with Joseph Priestley and Andrew Duncan, and on his own experiments in physics. Once again, Hope successfully raised the assafoetida plants (*Ferula persica* Willdenow) resulting from Pallas's travels, in the Royal Botanic Garden newly established at Edinburgh. In February 1783 he propagated the seed to 51 influential people living north and south of the border, including Sir Joseph Banks, president of the Royal Society. Hope's detailed account of the assafoetida plant, mentioning its medicinal properties and Guthrie's role, was published in the *Philosophical Transactions* for 1785.

Sir Alexander Crichton and Sir James Wylie

Alexander Crichton, descended from 'The Admirable Crichton' of the 16th century, was born at Newington in December 1763. He was apprenticed to the surgeon Alexander Wood, matriculated at Edinburgh University and attended lectures by John Hope, William Cullen, Joseph Black and Alexander Monro *secundus*. After graduating M.D. at Leyden in July 1785, Crichton studied at Paris, Stuttgart, Vienna, Halle, Berlin and Göttingen before taking up practice, as a doctor rather than a surgeon, in London. He was appointed physician to the Westminster Hospital in 1794. An important part of his work was as a lecturer in clinical studies, medicine, chemistry and materia medica.

A few years later Crichton became personal physician to the Duke of Cambridge. Prior to this he had already contributed to medical journals, establishing himself as a writer. In particular he distinguished himself by his book on *An Inquiry into the Nature and Origin of Mental Derangement*, published in 1798. Professor Dora B. Weiner has rightly drawn attention to this work, unusual for its emphasis on the physiological origins of mental illness. She points out that the eminent French psychiatrists, Philippe Pinel and Jeanne Étienne Esquirol, both regarded it very highly. Crichton's election to the Royal Society in May 1800 set the seal on his reputation.

In 1804 Crichton accepted the offer of physician-in-ordinary to Tsar Alexander I. A very popular figure at the Russian court, he also saw to the health of the Dowager Empress Marie.

Alexander Crichton was a very skilful chemist. He had demonstrated his analytical powers during his public lectures in London when, for instance, he elucidated a new theory of light and heat emitted in oxygen combustion, supported by experiments; and, as a further example, he had been asked to carry out tests on the medical effects of a substance invented by the chemist Richard Chenevix, compared with Dr James's similar, but more famous fever powder. Dr Matthew Halliday, born, like John Rogerson, at Lochbrow—in 1732—successfully administered the powder during the plague at Moscow and IAroslavl' in 1771. (In 1780 he was made director of the St Petersburg Inoculation Hospital founded by Catherine after Baron Dimsdale had inoculated her for smallpox. Halliday, who died at St Petersburg in 1809, personally inoculated all the imperial children.) Then, in 1807, Crichton and the apothecary, Konstantin Kirchov won the first prize offered by the Free Economic Society in St Petersburg for developing a method of refining vegetable oil, by using sulphuric acid, founding a refinery on Apothecaries' Island, in the Neva (where Robert Erskine had established the Apothecaries' Garden in 1714). One should also mention Crichton's innovatory pamphlet of 1817, *Experiments Made with the Vapour of Boiling Tar, in the Cure of Pulmonary Consumption*, in which he describes how he cured two patients of tuberculosis by treating them with fumes from tar.

Alexander Crichton had a very successful career in Russia, taking over the directorship of the country's Civil Medical Department. He dealt expeditiously with a major cholera outbreak in 1810 and vigorously tackled the problem of universal smallpox inoculation. His *Pharmacopoeia in usum nosocomii pauperum Petropolitani*, along the lines of the Edinburgh pauper's pharmacopoeia, was printed at the capital in 1807. He also found time to co-edit a two-volumed compendium on Russian medicine and the natural sciences. Published (1816 and 1817) in German, it is a fund of useful historical and up-to-date material on all aspects of these subjects.

Robert Dale Owen, in his autobiography, *Threading my Way*, mentions that it was Alexander Crichton who accompanied the Grand Duke Nicholas (later Nicholas I), as his physician and interpreter, when they stayed one night in December 1816 at Braxfield House, New Lanark, home of his father, Robert Owen. The socialist experimenter tactfully declined the Duke's offer to resettle two million of Britain's 'surplus' population in Russia in accordance with Malthusian principles! However, it is more likely to have been Alexander's nephew, Archibald William Crichton. He graduated at Edinburgh University in 1810 with an M.D. thesis dedicated to his uncle, joined the Russian service in 1811, distinguishing himself during the Napoleonic invasion, and was appointed physician to Grand Duke Nicholas in 1816. Like his uncle, he contributed articles to various medical journals, especially on cholera in Russia. When he accompanied the Grand Duke in 1819 on another visit to Britain, he was knighted, as Sir William Crichton, by the Prince Regent.

Crichton took an active interest in natural history. Elected a fellow of the Linnean Society of London in December 1793, he donated various items over the years, such as his translation from the German, in 1792, of J. F. Blumenbach's *Essay on Generation*; part of a large crystal of a Siberian emerald; a hedgehog; and the physician naturalist Langsdorff's account of his voyage around the world (1803-6) with Kruzenshtern—the first Russian circumnavigation. He also sent several consignments of Russian seed for cultivation at the Royal Botanical Garden in Kew. His preoccupation with materia medica is reflected by his membership of the Medico-Botanical Society. Both Crichton and James Wylie were elected foreign members of the Wernerian Natural History Society of Edinburgh in 1810 or 1811; and they and Crichton's nephew became honorary members in 1814 of the Royal Caledonian Horticultural Society, founded by Andrew Duncan, Matthew Guthrie's correspondent (Rogerson, too, was elected—in June 1817).

The Crichtons were a cultured family. Seven pictures from Alexander Crichton's own collection, previously in the Spanish Room at the Hermitage in Leningrad, are still exhibited in the museum's galleries. A keen mineralogist and geologist, Crichton was nominated member of the Geological Society of London in January 1811, and elected fellow on his return to Britain. He presented the Society with some Russian specimens and wrote several papers for its journal. Of special interest is an extract of a letter which he wrote from St Petersburg in August 1807 to Dr William Babington, one of the founders and, in 1822, president of the Geological Society, about two natural items that had just reached the Russian capital: a meteorite weighing 42 kg and an almost entirely preserved mammoth from Siberia (which may have been fetched by Adams, the British explorer, from the River Lena on the Arctic Ocean). Crichton's collection of minerals and previous stones, 'Formed with unremitting Attention and at unsparing Expense during Thirty Years,' was sold in 1827 (the sale lasted for sixteen days). It contained 2,600 items from all over Russia and from other countries, many of them extremely rare and valuable. Crichton was a friend of the eminent French mineralogist, the Comte de Bournon. In the catalogue that the Count made of his own collection in 1813, he acknowledged receiving Siberian minerals from Crichton, 'aussi bon minéraliste qu'il est grand médicin et excellent chimiste', and named a crystal 'Crichtonite' in his honour.

James Wylie, whose death in 1854 ended the 150-year dynasty of Scottish doctors in Russia, was born at Kincardine-on-Forth in 1768, studied medicine at Edinburgh, and entered the Russian service as a surgeon in the Eletsky regiment at the end of 1790. After obtaining an M.D. by diploma from Aberdeen University in December 1794, he left the army to become medical attendant to a prince, engaging also in private practice at Moscow or St Petersburg. Wylie owed his appointment at the Russian court to his surgical skill and boldness: when Rogerson and Beck, a German surgeon, were in despair about using a catheter to extract a stone from the urinary bladder of Baron Otto Blom, Danish ambassador to the Russian court, Rogerson remembered his compatriot. Wylie

Sir James Wylie.

managed to improvise a trocar from the catheter and was able to perform the lithotomy, saving the life of the envoy, a friend of the emperor. As a result he was appointed court operator on 25 February 1798. In July of the following year he became the Tsar's personal surgeon for saving the life of another of the monarch's friends, Count A. P. Kutaizov, by carrying out the first laryngotomy operation in Russia on him. Soon afterwards the Medical College confirmd Wylie's qualifications as a doctor and surgeon in Russia, making him its honorary member. On 24 March 1801 when Paul was strangled with a scarf, three Scottish doctors—Wylie, Guthrie and Grieve—performed the autopsy and embalmed the body, Wylie giving out that he had succumbed to an apoplexy.

From January 1806 until 1854, James Wylie was Chief Medical Inspector of the Army. Upon the separation of the military from the civilian, in 1811, he also directed the Medical Department of the War Ministry (until 1836)—with Alexander Crichton in charge of the Civil Medical Department and (Sir) James Leighton, grandfather of the painter, Sir Frederick Leighton, shouldering responsibility for the country's naval medicine! At the same time Wylie was president of the Medico-Chirurgical Academy at St Petersburg, with a branch at Moscow, for training surgeons and doctors, from 1808 to 1838; so that, effectively, he was head of all Russia's military medical services. As such, he showed a real genius for administration, reforming and, in many cases, creating army medicine in Russia. He introduced numerous precepts; his handbook on surgical operations, printed in 1806, was the first to be published in Russian; he founded a military medical journal in 1808 (the second Russian-language medical one); and in the same year Wylie brought out his Russian military pharmacopoeia, the *Pharmacopoeia castrensis ruthena*, representing three years' work by its compiler and unusual in its relatively full coverage of pharmacy and pharmacognosy, and the adoption of the new pharmaceutical nomenclature. Known as *Pharmacopoeia castrensis Wylie*, it ran through four editions and was replaced only in 1866.

In 1805 the Emperor Alexander ordered Wylie 'to make out preventative and curative instructions for the Russian Troops in Corfu and the other Greek islands threatened from their situation' with yellow fever, or the 'new American Plague' (Matthew Guthrie, in his 'Supplementary Tour'). The result was Wylie's book, dedicated to Alexander and printed in Russian by the Medical Press at St Petersburg in 1805, *On the Yellow American Fever*. It provides a short historical account, followed by a comprehensive discussion of the disease, with clear recommendations for its prevention and treatment. Some twenty years later saw the publication of another work in Russian by Wylie—his *Practical Remarks on the Plague*—together with a translation of James Johnson's influential book on *The Influence of Tropical Climate on European Constitutions*.

Wylie accompanied Paul and Alexander on most of their journeys and all their campaigns. He took part in the wars of 1805 and 1826 (Russo-Turkish), but especially distinguished himself during the Napoleonic Wars: at the Battle of Bordino (1812), when he is mentioned by Tolstoy, in *War and Peace* (as 'Villier', the French pronunciation of his name in Russia), he is said to have performed 200 operations on the field; and at Dresden (1813) he amputated General Moreau's legs, shattered by a cannon-shot as he was talking to the Tsar. Wylie himself was wounded three times. He received decorations and awards from four Russian sovereigns and numerous potentates, Napoleon among them. Both he and Alexander Crichton became honorary members of the Russian Imperial Academy of Sciences. In 1814 Wylie accompanied Alexander on a visit to England and was knighted by the Prince Regent, on Ascot Heath, improvising with a Cossack ataman's sword. At the Tsar's special request, he was also created a baronet. In Paris after the British visit, Alexander himself designed a coat-of-arms for Wylie, confirmed by George III in 1819 as a favour to the Tsar.

Tsar Alexander I died, 48 years old, of a fever at Taganrog in south Russia on 19 November 1825. Although Wylie's diary, written in French and printed as a calendar in 1825, only gives very brief details of the Tsar's last illness, it indicates the frustration caused by his refusal to have any medication until it was too late. Wylie's full report on Alexander's illness and death, thought to have been lost, has been rediscovered and presents a much fuller picture, together with an autopsy report signed by him and eight other doctors or surgeons. It was originally written in Latin and then translated into German. An edition, with a commentary on it, has been planned for a German medical history journal. However, very strong rumours still persist that Alexander did not die in 1825

The statue of Sir James Wylie in the grounds of the hospital he founded in St Petersburg.

but lived on as a hermit in Siberia for nearly another 40 years. The author of an article in a Cologne newspaper in 1933 claimed that Wylie's 'Memoirs', lately found among the Imperial Secret Archives, provided documentary evidence of Alexander's survival. They showed, he wrote, that the body of a courier, killed in an accident a few days earlier, was embalmed while the Tsar, by arrangement with Wylie, boarded an English ship at Taganrog, on the Sea of Azov on the night of 18/19 November 1825. In 1841, the article continues, Nicholas I asked Wylie, sworn to secrecy, to write a single copy of his 'Memoirs' of the happenings. Each Tsar, as was clear from the notes and signatures on the manuscript, undertook to reveal the true course of the events to his successor when he came of age. The last signatures, according to the writer of this article, were those of Tsar Nicholas II and his brother, Grand Duke Michael.

James Wylie's death in 1854 marks the end of an era. The most 'russified' of Scottish doctors, he left the bulk of his considerable fortune for the building of a large hospital in St Petersburg, called the Michael Clinical Hospital of Baronet Wylie. An impressive statue unveiled in his honour in 1859 at the front of the hospital, was transferred in 1950 to a small garden at the back of the building in Leningrad. Beside the helmet at his feet is a copy of his pharmacopoeia.

From this survey it will have been seen that Scottish doctors and surgeons performed a dynamic and pioneering role in Russia from the beginning of the 18th to the middle of the 19th centuries. Well placed and qualified as intermediaries, they channelled and reflected back to Britain very wide and varied information about Russian medicine, natural history and culture—itself an invaluable contribution to Scottish-Russian relations.

SELECT BIBLIOGRAPHY

A. GENERAL

J. H. Appleby, 'British Doctors in Russia, 1657-1807; their Contribution to Anglo-Russian Medical and Natural History'. University of East Anglia thesis, June 1979 (Copy in the National Library of Scotland).

Judith Burgen, *Medical Adventurers in Tsarist Russia*. To be published in 1987-8.

B. INDIVIDUAL MEDICAL MEN

1. *Robert Erskine*

John H. Appleby, 'Robert-Erskine—Scottish pioneer of Russian natural history'. *Archives of Natural History*, 1, no. 3 (1982), 377-98.

John H. Appleby and Andrew Cunningham, 'Robert Erskine and Archibald Pitcairne—two Scottish physicians' outstanding libraries', *The Bibliotheck*, 11, no. 1 (1982), 3-16.

Rev. Robert Paul, 'Letters and documents relating to Robert Erskine...' *Miscellany of the Scottish Historical Society*, 44, no. 2 (1904), 373-430.

2. *Thomas Garvine*

Renate Burgess, 'Thomas Garvine—Ayrshire surgeon active in Russia', *Medical History*, 19, no. 1 (1975), 91-4 (plus portrait).

3. *John Bell*

J. L. Stevenson's introduction in *A journey from St Petersburg to Pekin*, Edinburgh, 1965.

4. *James Mounsey*

John H. Appleby, '"Rhubarb" Mounsey and the Surinam toad—a Scottish physician-naturalist in Russia', *Archives of Natural History*, 11, no. 1 (1982), 137-52.

R. W. Innes Smith, 'Dr James Mounsey of Rammerscales', *Edinburgh Medical Journal*, 33 (1926), 272-279.

5. *John Rogerson*

Anthony G. Cross, 'John Rogerson: physician to Catherine the Great', *Canadian Slavic Studies*, 4, no. 3 (1970), 594-601.

6. John Grieve

John H. Appleby, 'John Grieve's correspondence with Joseph Black and some contemporaneous Russo-Scottish medical intercommunication', *Medical History*, 29, no. 4 (1985), 401-13.

7. Matthew Guthrie

John H. Appleby, 'St Petersburg to Edinburgh—Matthew Guthrie's introduction of medicinal plants in the context of Scottish-Russian natural history exchange', *Archives of Natural History*, 13, no. 1 (1987), 28-40.

A. G. Cross, 'Arcticus and "The Bee" (1790-4): an episode in Anglo-Russian cultural relations', *Oxford Slavonic Papers*, New Series, 2 (1969), 62-76.

K. A. Papmehl, 'Matthew Guthrie—the forgotten student of 18th-century Russia', *Canadian Slavonic Papers*, 11, no. 2 (1969), 166-81.

Jessie M. Sweet, 'Matthew Guthrie (1743-1807): an eighteenth-century gemmologist', *Annals of Science*, 20, no. 4 (1964), 245-302.

8. Sir Alexander Crichton

Dictionary of National Biography, v. 13, 85-6.

E. M. Tansey, 'The life and works of Sir Alexander Crichton, F.R.S. (1763-1856): a Scottish physician to the Imperial Russian Court', *Notes and Records of the Royal Society of London*, 38, no. 2 (1984), 241-59.

9. Sir James Wylie

Dictionary of National Biography, v. 63, 236.

Heinz Müller-Dietz, 'When did Alexander I of Russia die?' *Sydsvenska Medicinhistoriska Sällskapets Årsskrift*, 22 (1987) (in English).

John B. Wilson, 'Three Scots in the service of the Czars'. *The Practitioner*, April and May, 210 (1973), 569-74, and 704-8 (*Wylie*, *Rogerson* and *Mounsey*).

FROM THE BANKS OF THE NEVA TO THE SHORES OF LAKE BAIKAL: SOME ENTERPRISING SCOTS IN RUSSIA

JOHN R. BOWLES

EARLIER chapters have illustrated the growth of contacts between Scotland and Russia and especially the importance of the contributions made by Scots to Russia's development. These growing contacts reached their peak, as Professor Cross has shown in his chapter, in the reign of Catherine the Great. This essay, largely based on a variety of secondary sources, sets out to illustrate the achievements of some of those Scots (all of them, incidentally, hailing from the Lowlands) who were active in Russia towards the end of the 18th and during the first half of the 19th centuries.

A key figure in the careers of several Scots dealt with in this essay is that of Charles Gascoigne (of mixed Scots-English origin) who was Managing Director of the Carron Company from 1769 to 1786. The Carron Company, founded in 1759 on the River Carron near Falkirk, was the largest ironworks in Scotland. Its commercial links with Russia dated from the early 1770s, when it had begun to export cannon and guns to meet the needs of Russia's reviving navy. The Russian navy at that time contained a strong British element as it was headed by Admiral Knowles until 1774 and by the Scottish Admiral Samuel Greig until his death in 1788.

There were often problems with these early shipments of cannon to Russia since they frequently did not meet the required standards: similar failures occurred in other countries, too, at that time, due to imperfect understanding of the new techniques that were necessary. However, the Company was involved in a more successful Scoto-Russian enterprise which began in 1774. In that year a team of Carron workmen (including W. Bruce, D. Conochie, J. Ditchburn, J. Martin, J. Rennie, J. Smith, A. Thomson and a Mr Taylor) left for Russia under the leadership of one Adam Smith (not the author of *The Wealth of Nations*) to install a steam-powered water-pump in the dry dock at Kronshtadt, the island naval base and port guarding the approaches to St Petersburg. Both Knowles and Greig, as successive governors of the island, were keen to improve its facilities. The Carron men supervised 150 Russian workers in a project which lasted almost three years. In June 1777 they started up a 77 horse power machine (relatively powerful for its time), which enabled two pumps to pump out 976 cubic metres of water an hour. Most of the Carron men returned home after the completion of their task but Adam Smith and William Bruce remained behind. They took Russian citizenship and signed contracts to train Russian workers in the new technology of steam power. Moreover, Russians began to be sent to Britain for experience in this field and the first such trainee arrived at the Carron works in 1779.

Thus, despite the initial problems of defective cannon, useful contacts with Russia had been established by Carron which Gascoigne continued to develop. With the resolution of many of the earlier technical problems, guns began to be exported to Russia in considerable quantities; one consignment alone in 1784 was valued at £3,400. However, Gascoigne, an ambitious and energetic entrepreneur with few apparent scruples, began to run into trouble with both his colleagues at Carron and with the British government. Whilst Carron's export of guns was legal, the dispatch of patterns for the moulding of guns and for boring machinery, which was sanctioned by Gascoigne and which might have given Russia an independent gun-making capacity, was definitely illegal at that time, and caused him to be summoned before the Lord Advocate. He ruled that Gascoigne had acted outside the law but should be pardoned because of ignorance and his co-operation with the enquiry. His personal financial situation, however, was now precarious. Though still managing director, his shares were held in trust for outside creditors and he also owed large sums to the Company itself.

Russia's need of technical expertise in weapons production gave Gascoigne the opportunity to make a fresh start. At the invitation of Greig, who had secured official backing for a new cannon foundry based on the advanced Carron techniques, and of the Empress Catherine herself, he left Scotland for good in 1786. He took with him some machinery and a small group of specialists and workmen but left behind considerable debts which were never repaid. From his arrival in Russia until his death in 1806, he headed the Aleksandrovsk Cannon Factory and the Koncherzersk Foundry at Petrozavodsk on Lake Onega, some two hundred miles north-east of St Petersburg. During his time in charge both factories were reconstructed. Advanced machines and equipment were put into operation and foreign specialists attracted to work there. His activities, though, were not confined to these enterprises. 'Combining technical expertise and entrepreneurial skills with the determined pursuit of his own interest', he had a finger in many pies. He was responsible for a small iron foundry built at Kronshtadt in 1789 which produced grenades, shells and shot, and was the first in Russia to use scrap metal as its basic raw material, while another foundry, established under his auspices (near the Narva Gate on the south-west side of St Petersburg in 1801) was the forerunner of the famous Putilov (now Kirov) works. In the 1790s he served as consultant for Admiral Mordvinov's reconstruction of the docks at Nikolaev, on the River Bug, and he was also largely responsible for the statute on weights and measures issued by the Russian government in 1797. The new weights and measures were at first manufactured exclusively at Gascoigne's Petrozavodsk works, and it was due to him that the inch was chosen as the basis of calculation for the Russian arshin.

Charles Gascoigne.

His personal fortune grew steadily as his interests expanded. His original employment contract stipulated that his salary should be paid at a fixed rate of exchange and thus protected him from the adverse effects of currency fluctuations. Having entered the official state service, he attained the rank of Actual State Councillor by 1798. The Emperor Paul granted him 2,000 serfs, while his second marriage (to the daughter of the Scottish doctor, Matthew Guthrie, then working in St Petersburg) did nothing to hinder his advance, since she apparently became the mistress of Procurator-General

Lopukhin, the father of the Emperor's favourite, thus providing him with a channel of influence to the highest authorities.

In his later years in Russia, Gascoigne became director of a large textile-mill at Aleksandrovsk, near the capital, which proved to be another lucrative position. He also began the reconstruction of the Izhora works at Kolpino, south of St Petersburg, for which the plans had been drawn up by the Scottish architect, William Hastie. By the time of his death in 1806, Gascoigne had amassed a considerable fortune, though still managing to owe the state considerable sums of money which were only finally written off by the Russian government, following the petition of his eldest daughter, Anna, Dowager Countess of Haddington, in 1825.

A balanced evaluation of Gascoigne's achievements in Russia is difficult to make especially as his own self-interest was such a powerful motivating force. He introduced advanced western technology into Russia as well as bringing to the county skilled English and Scottish workmen, although as Russian writers have pointed out, this was sometimes at the cost of neglecting well-trained Russian ones. The costs involved were sometimes huge as Gascoigne frequently went over budget, and though the works at Petrozavodsk became a kind of 'showcase' of the best current industrial practice, they were rather isolated from the rest of Russian industry. Yet here, and in the other enterprises with which he was associated, modern techniques and skilled labour forces did take root and develop in a way that was to be fruitful for Russia's future progress. His career in Russia has been summed up in this way by E. Robinson:

Much as he was envied and disliked by British and Russian alike, his energy and technical 'know-how' were respected and he was known to have a hand in every mechanical development worth mentioning during his twenty years in Russia ... it must be said that the arming of the Russian forces in this period would have been far less efficient had it not been for Gascoigne's expertise in cannon production. ...

As an individual he seems to have been less attractive—'he hid the unacceptable face of capitalism behind the smile of the captain of industry, courtier and noble gentleman', is the verdict of R. P. Bartlett.

Scottish influence on Russian industry remained strong even after Gascoigne's death, as several of his enterprises were subsequently run by his fellow-countrymen. Alexander Wilson succeeded him as director of the Kolpino ironworks and the Aleksandrovsk textile-mill (though not receiving Gascoigne's high salary and other benefits), while Adam Armstrong took over control of the Petrozavodsk factories in 1807.

Armstrong was born near Jedburgh in 1762 and after studying at Edinburgh University was expected to follow a career in the Church. Instead, he took a post as tutor to the children of Admiral Greig and found himself in Russia. He played a part in the recruiting of Gascoigne and, as one of his aides, entered the ranks of the government service, rising to become a collegiate assessor and, in 1798, one of the managerial team at the Petrozavodsk complex. He was promoted to be Gascoigne's successor over the head of the Deputy Director Poltoratskii who, according to one view, was much the better qualified man. Indeed, he may have obtained the post through favouritism and patronage in high places, since he does not seem to have had any technical education though he must have picked up a great deal of practical experience through working with Gascoigne. However, he does seem to have been a competent administrator and remained as director until his death in 1818. Output and quality were maintained and he was able to effect considerable cost reductions through the discovery of new deposits of fire clay for the furnaces and the substitution of pinewood as fuel, instead of expensive imported coal.

The lot of the average factory worker, who was usually a peasant attached for most of his working life to a particular enterprise, was not an enviable one at this time, and Armstrong's treatment of his workforce has received varying assessments from Russian commentators. Some speak of his having won the trust and affection of his employees through the trouble he took over their welfare. Others criticize him, and Gascoigne before him, for sometimes forcing the workers to labour round-the-clock and on holidays in order to maximize profits.

Armstrong was involved in an incident, recounted by the Russian historian Balagurov, which casts a sombre light on the treatment of the lower classes at this period. At the beginning of August 1810, Mariai Gerasimova, a servant girl in the house of the British mining surveyor Clark was found to have hung herself. Apparently she had been ill-treated by Clark and his wife and had several times threatened 'to do something to herself'. She had been beaten with a stick by Clark on the day of her death. The police and a Dr Neiman, who examined the corpse, found spots of blood on her body but 'omitted' to mention what had caused them. The military tribunal of the Petrozavodsk factories decided that Gerasimova had killed herself 'from deep-rooted malice and ignorance, vices not infrequently met with in people of her situation'. As Factory Director, Armstrong upheld the decision and the matter was closed. Shortly afterwards the body of one of the British specialists was found near Petrozavodsk but all investigations into the affair proved fruitless.

A happier light is shed by Armstrong's daughter-in-law who, in her will, left three thousand rubles to the poorest workers of the Aleksandrovsk Factory in his memory. One of his sons, Roman Adamovich Armstrong, also enjoyed a notable career. Like his father he was educated at Edinburgh University. He returned to Russia in 1811 and entered the Department of Mines. He took Russian citizenship and rose to become the Director of Mines at the Petrozavodsk factories before moving to take over the direction of the Mint at St Petersburg (1843-1858). He ended his career with the rank of Lieutenant-General of Mines and died in 1864.

As mentioned previously, while Armstrong succeeded Gascoigne at Petrozavodsk in the north, two of Gascoigne's posts in the St Petersburg area were taken over by Alexander Wilson. Wilson's father James, an Edinburgh smith, had come to Russia, not with Gascoigne, but with the group of Scottish workmen recruited by the architect Charles Cameron in 1784 to help in his work for the Empress Catherine. He moved to an arms factory in Sestroretsk, on the Gulf of Finland, in 1790. The young Alexander grew up speaking fluent Russian and in the 1790s became Gascoigne's aide and interpreter. He rose to become Assistant Director at the large Aleksandrovsk textile mill in 1803 and was also depute to Gascoigne during the reconstruction of the Izhora works at Kolpino. Following Gascoigne's death in 1806, he assumed control of both enterprises and one of his first tasks was to deal with the problems caused by the bursting of the new works' dam at Kolpino, only a month after its reopening. Repairs were costly but the new factory was soon operating satisfactorily.

Wilson served the Russian state for fifty years in these posts in which he rose to the rank of Engineer-General and received numerous decorations, including the order of Aleksandr Nevskii. He made several return visits to Britain to keep abreast of the latest technical developments and to invite specialists to Russia to train Russian workmen. His character displays a marked contrast to that of Gascoigne. He lacked the latter's drive and dynamism (and greed) and appears to have been less of an innovator, but he was honest, respected and well-liked. The distinguished engineer, Sir John Rennie, visited Wilson on a trip to Russia and portrayed him affectionately in his autobiography:

Engineer-General Alexander Wilson in the uniform he so disliked wearing.

He possessed a calm even temper, firm, but just, and conciliating, with a competent knowledge of what he undertook to perform, without possessing any considerable amount of invention . . . [he] was thoroughly liked and respected, from the humblest workman under his orders up to the Emperor who was very fond of him. Lastly, he was thoroughly honest, a rare thing in Russia in these days, where peculation was rife from the highest to the lowest; and if Wilson had followed the universal example, which he might have done with impunity, he would have made a large fortune, but after many year's service he died comparatively poor. . . . All persons employed like Wilson had military rank; he concealed this as much as he could; but in St Petersburg he was always obliged to wear uniform, and as there were guard houses in almost every street, wherever he passed the guard turned out to salute him, which annoyed him much.

The Alexandrovsk textile mill became, under Wilson, a regular visiting place for many western travellers including the Marquis de Custine (author of the famous *La Russie en 1839*), and John Quincy Adams (the first American ambassador to Russia). It seems to have been a model of its kind producing not only cotton but linen, quilts, sail-cloth table-cloths and Russia's total output of playing-cards. A third of its workforce consisted of orphan children from the St Petersburg Foundling Home, who were obviously a form of cheap labour, yet visitors (Adams excepted) judged their conditions of employment exemplary. 'I will venture to affirm, that healthier, better clothed and more orderly children are not to be seen in any institution', commented William Rae Wilson in his *Travels in Russia* (1828), while the Rev. R. Lister Venables in his *Domestic Scenes in Russia* (1839) wrote: 'This, like all other public establishments such as barracks and hospitals, which I have seen in this country, appears a perfect model of order and cleanliness; a fact which is the more striking in Russia, since there is often abundant room for improvement in these respects in private houses.' Wilson took a well-earned retirement in 1856 and died in 1866 at the age of 90.

Important as the contributions made by Wilson and the Armstrongs were to Russia's industrial development, the greatest impact was made by another of the Carron men who came over with Gascoigne. This was Charles Baird who was

Charles Baird.

born at Westertown in the parish of Borthkenner, near Carron, on 20 December 1766. He was the second of seven sons of Nicol Baird (Superintendent of the Forth and Clyde Canal) and Christian Pringle. He had five years' schooling in Edinburgh before starting as an apprentice at the Carron Works, where he rose to become head of the casting and finishing ordnance by the time of his departure for Russia.

He helped Gascoigne in the reconstruction of the Petrozavodsk factories before striking out on his own. He went into partnership with an English instrument-maker Francis Morgan, who had already worked for some twenty years in St Petersburg, to supply and maintain factory machinery. After marrying Morgan's daughter he eventually inherited the whole business, but by then he had already begun to build his own ironworks and create a considerable industrial empire. Baird's works soon grew to be one of the largest in Russia though they actually contravened a ban on industrial development within the capital. His general usefulness to the state and willingness to train workers seconded by the government told in his favour.

Baird resembled Gascoigne in his energy, shrewdness and love of money. His interests were similarly wide-ranging, and he had a special talent for picking up useful new British inventions, patenting them in Russia and enjoying the benefits of the subsequent monopolies. He built a saw-mill, a steam-operated flour-mill, machines for the Russian Mint and the Arsenal, as well as a sugar-refinery. This latter enterprise was especially lucrative as the German traveller J. G. Kohl noted:

Mr Beart's [i.e. Baird's] sugar-manufactory is not shown to anyone, because the great demand for its produce is the result of a secret—the discovery of a substitute for bullock's blood in purifying sugar. The Russians, namely during fast-time, deny themselves the use of this article from overstrained religious scruples, on account of the small portion of animal matter which may be left in it when refined by the usual process. At such time, therefore, no sugar but that which is provided with the stamp of Beart's manufactory is brought to table, because it is well known that in his mode of refining no animal substance is employed. Beart's sugar, of course, goes to all parts of Russia and considerable quantities of it are met with at all the fairs in the interior.

With his nephew, William Handyside, as his right-hand technical expert, Baird was at the forefront of many technological developments. On 4 November 1815, practically the whole population of the island of Kronshtadt assembled to witness the arrival from St Petersburg of what was one of the wonders of its day—the *Elizaveta*, Russia's first steamship, built by Baird. The *Elizaveta* consisted of a balance steam engine of the Watt system fitted onto an ordinary Tikhvinskii barge with a brick chimney for a funnel. It was neither particularly fast (about six miles an hour) nor comfortable, but it won for Baird a monopoly of the freight and passenger traffic between the capital and Kronshtadt. This did not escape the notice of William Rae Wilson, cited earlier for his view of the orphan children at Alexander Wilson's textile mill, who travelled on one of Baird's boats. He wrote:

We proceeded in a steam-boat for which the proprietor Mr Baird, a Scotchman, who has resided here some time, and who, in the language of his native country, found this concern to be a 'dripping roast' has obtained a patent for a term of years—a favour that is looked upon with an eye of jealousy by the Russians. Some idea may be formed of the profits of this concern when I state that, according to our information, the proprietor had made 70,000 rubles in the course of one week by conveying passengers to Peterhof at the time of a fete.

Baird's factories left a considerable physical imprint on St Petersburg as they produced the iron and other metalwork for buildings throughout the city. Many of the intricate iron railings surrounding churches, palaces and bridges were also cast in his factories. The ironwork for St Pantaleimon's Bridge over the Fontanka (designed by G. Traitteur and V. Khristianovich), which was Russia's first suspension bridge open for vehicular traffic (1823), was supplied by Baird who also devised a hydraulic chain tester that met with Traitteur's warm approval. However, the two biggest projects that Baird (and his son Francis) were involved with were the Alexander Column and St Isaac's Cathedral. The Alexander Column, designed by the French architect Montferrand in memory of Tsar Alexander I and the victories over Napoleon, consisted of a giant granite monolith on a base, surmounted by the figure of an angel holding a cross. The four bas-reliefs at the foot of the column, the four eagles at the angle of the pedestal, the bronze railing round the monument, the four eighteen-feet-high candelabra outside the corners of the railings, and the huge figure of the angel holding a cross more than twenty feet high at its summit were all produced, to Montferrand's designs, in a specially built foundry at the Baird works.

Kohl visited the foundry during his travels and admired the model of the angel—'which appeared to us colossal, rising as it does through two stories of the building while that on the top of the column, of the very same size, is scarcely noticed by the spectator who views it from below'.

The Baird works also supplied much of the metalwork for St Isaac's, it, too, designed by Montferrand. The dome of the cathedral alone required about one thousand tons of cast iron, five hundred tons of wrought iron, three hundred tons of bronze, fifty tons of copper and two hundred and fifty pounds of gold. Among the other pieces of work completed for a building which was intended to rival St Peter's in Rome,

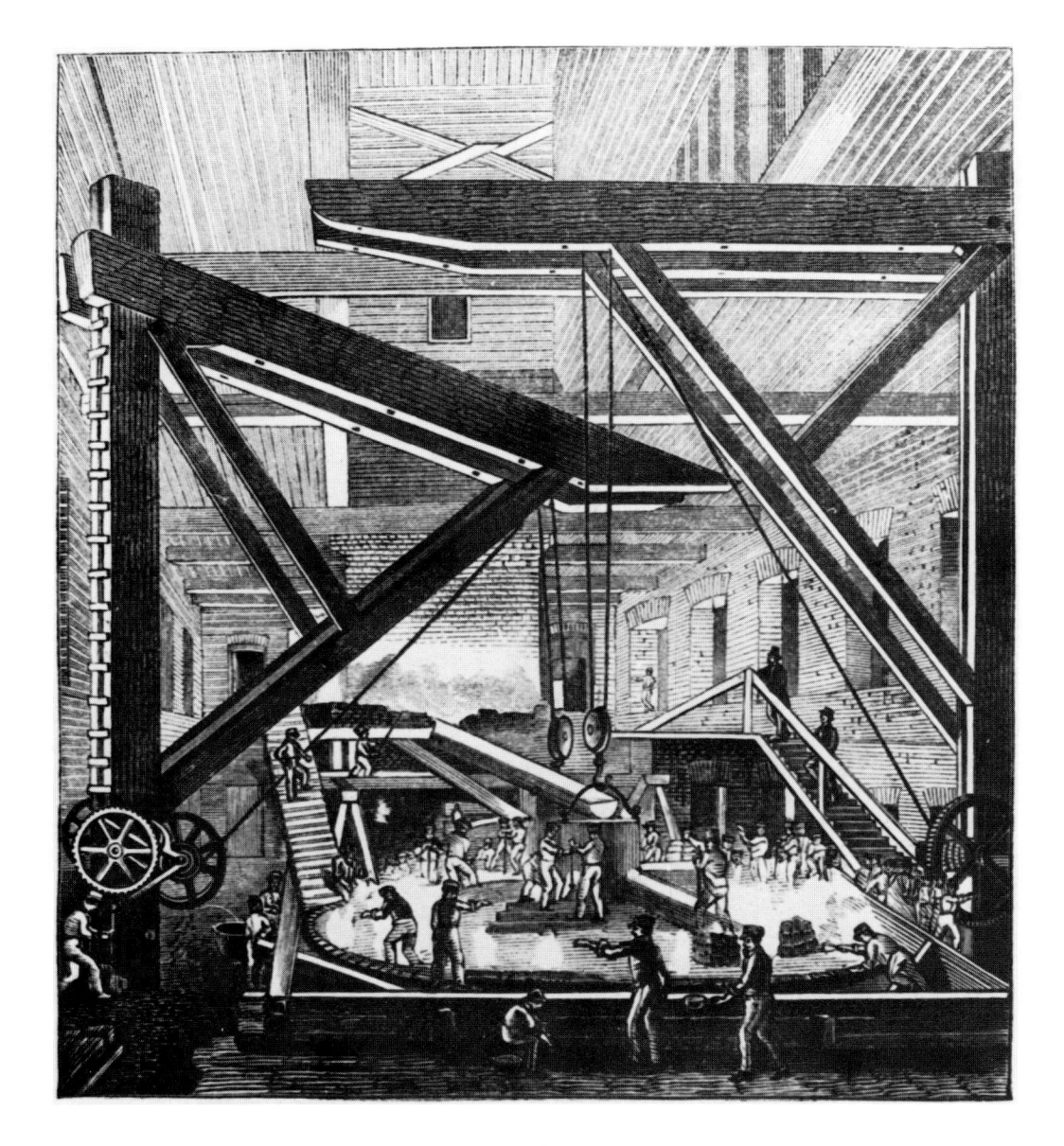

An interior view of the Baird works.

St Issac's Cathedral with the four bas-reliefs cast in the Baird works (opposite).

73

were four bas-reliefs, cast in bronze and weighing about eighty tons each, for the four fronts of the cathedral and twelve fifteen feet high bronze figures of the Apostles. The Baird works became a byword for efficiency in St Petersburg. The expression 'kak u Berda na zavode' ('just like at Baird's factory') was, for a time, a catch-phrase in the capital, having the meaning that something was being run smoothly. The works enjoyed Imperial patronage and were visited by three successive Emperors (Alexander I, Nicholas I and Alexander II), and both Charles and his son Francis were awarded orders of merit including those of St Anne, St Stanislav and St Vladimir.

Like Gascoigne, however, Baird was regarded in a somewhat equivocal light by his contemporaries. E. Robinson quotes from a letter written by an English engineer, Zacchaeus Walker, then working in St Petersburg, to his uncle, the industrialist Matthew Boulton:

He is about 40 years of age,—certainly very active and intelligent,—knows the Russian language well,—which, rest assured is a very essential point and a work of time:—is pretty intimately acquainted with the mechanical professors in general, both Russian and Foreigners—also with many of the principal nobility; and with the proper mode of applying the key to the private doors of the Chief Officers in most of the Government Departments; and as you will have observed, comes from the North side of the Tweed which is the best recommendation a man can bring to this city, the Caledonian Phalanx being the strongest and most numerous, and moving always in the closest union. If not secured as a friend, he is in my estimation, the person who by his experience and address might in the event of your engaging extensively in this country, become the most troublesome opponent.

The kindly Sir John Rennie, who encountered Baird, as well as Wilson, on his Russian journey comes to a more generous conclusion about him. While recognising his devotion to money-making and his willingness to use whatever methods necessary to secure government contracts, he comments:

… and we must not omit to mention that Baird, whilst benefiting himself, was of the greatest service to Russia, and tended materially to advance her prosperity by the numerous valuable inventions he introduced, and by training the natives, and inciting them and urging them to make all sorts of improvements, which, without such a man, would never have been undertaken, so that nobody grudged his wealth, and he left the country to which he had been a real benefactor universally liked and esteemed.

Charles' son, Francis, was educated at Edinburgh University, and joined him in the business at the age of seventeen. He managed the works after his father's retirement and became sole proprietor on his death in 1843. Apart from his involvement in the construction of the Alexander Column and of St Isaac's Cathedral, which has already been mentioned, the most notable project with which he was connected was the erection of the Blagoveshchensk (Annunciation) Bridge. This

Francis Baird.

The railings of the Blagoveshchensk Bridge which were cast in the Baird works.

was the first permanent metal bridge over the Neva (at its completion it was, for a short time, the longest cast-iron arch structure in the world). Under the direction of its Russian designer Kerbedz, construction lasted from 1843 to 1850. Baird was responsible for the casting of the intricate iron railings (designed by Alexander Briullov), and of some of the parts of the swinging span section of the bridge, which had to be raised to allow the passage of shipping. The bridge, now named the Lieutenant Schmidt bridge, after a revolutionary hero, was replaced by a steel structure in the 1930s though the original railings have been restored. Under Francis Baird the total workforce of the firm grew to some 1,500 employees but, after his death in 1864, a series of mergers which led to the formation, in 1880, of the Usines Franco-Russes (Baird) conglomerate, brought the distinctive Baird industrial empire to an end.

It would seem appropriate briefly to mention here the contribution made by another Scot, Matthew Clark (or Clarke) to the physical appearance of the capital. The son of one of the original members of Gascoigne's Carron group, he headed the state ironworks at a site not far from Baird's, and for more than a quarter of a century acted as a government consultant and supplier of ironwork and machinery for public buildings. He worked closely with the architects Rossi and Stasov on a series of major construction projects including the Narva Gate, the General Staff building on Palace Square, the Alexandrinsky (now Pushkin) Theatre, and the reconstruction of the Winter Palace after the fire of 1837.

At the same time as members of the 'Caledonian Phalanx' in the capital were making substantial contributions to Russia's material development, other groups of Scots, far away on the periphery of the Empire, were endeavouring to change the spiritual allegiance of some of her many non-Russian subjects. In the Caucasus and Siberia, Scottish missionaries were engaged on an improbable and heroic, if ultimately futile, attempt to evangelize some of the non-Christian peoples of the Russian Empire.

In 1802 the Edinburgh Missionary Society obtained, from Tsar Alexander I, a grant of some eighteen thousand acres of land for a missionary station in the foothills of the Caucasus. The Tsar was keen to establish foreign settlements in the newly-conquered borderland regions of his Empire as part of a general policy of pacification, but the reasons for the Society's decision are not quite so clear. There seems to have been a belief that the Caucasus region, on the boundary between Europe and Asia, offered the prospect of a large number of conversions among the surrounding non-Christian populations. Whatever the precise reasons, the first missionaries arrived at Karass, some 25 miles from the town of Georgievsk, to found a small Scottish colony which survived for more than three decades among the Circassian tribesmen. A charter granted by the government in 1806 gave the colony several important privileges, including a thirty-year immunity from taxation and the right to internal self-government. The most significant one, however, was the right to purchase enslaved Tatar children, with a view to educating them as Christians. The only proviso was that they should eventually, at the age of 23, have the right to buy their own freedom and leave the colony.

The colony's population was never large; in the years up to 1813 when the Reverend Henry Brunton, one of the founder members, died, 23 people had been sent out from Edinburgh of whom almost a half had perished (the early years had seen outbreaks of dysentery and the plague). Even allowing for the birth of several children the total number of colonists never exceeded 30, and they were greatly out-numbered by the arrival, in 1809, of a group of more than one hundred German immigrants from the province of Saratov, who settled down alongside the Scots. They seem to have co-existed amicably enough but the administrative burden on the missionary leaders was substantially increased.

For three decades the missionaries were occupied in cultivating the land and administering the settlement, in learning the local languages and translating the scriptures, as well as in educating the ransomed children and undertaking evangelizing tours among some of the neighbouring tribes. Branches of the mission were established at Orenburg, on the southern edge of the Urals, and at Astrakhan, where the Volga flows into the Caspian Sea, in 1815. However, any evangelizing dynamism had clearly been exhausted by the 1820s and when the Society (now renamed the Scottish Missionary Society) closed the mission in 1833, the number of permanent converts to Christianity totalled just nine.

Several factors mitigated against the success of the mission. The sporadic outbreaks of violence among the recently-conquered tribes required the permanent stationing of a detachment of Cossacks in the settlement. While this brought increased security for the colonists, it placed a barrier between the missionaries and the local inhabitants which complicated relations between them. The missionaries were also handicapped by having to devote so much time to the material problems concerned with the running of the colony that the amount left over for purely missionary work was greatly reduced. Although they made considerable progress in mastering the local language, their unfamiliarity with Arabic was a serious disadvantage. Dr Ebenezer Henderson, born near Dunfermline and a leading figure in the short-lived Russian Bible Society, noted in his book *Biblical Researches and Travels in Russia* (1826), that:

One radical defect in the qualifications of the Missionaries hitherto sent out by the Society (Mr Brunton excepted) is unquestionably their ignorance of the Arabic language. This has been most severely felt by such of them as are otherwise well qualified for the work to which they have been called, and they now seek to repair it by sacrificing a portion of their precious missionary time to the acquirement of a critical acquaintance with the original of the Koran, an evil which might have been prevented by timely attention to the subject previous to their leaving Britain. What should we think of a Mohammedan Effendi, who should settle in any part of Scotland and attempt to convince the inhabitants that the doctrines of the Bible were false, and yet knew nothing of the languages in which it was written?

It was the strength of Islam which was, in fact, the main obstacle in the way of the missionaries' hopes of mass conversions. They found it difficult to refute a faith which did not deny the existence of Christ, but merely allotted him a subordinate role in the scheme of things. Islam, moreover, had both a religious and cultural hold on the local tribes as a symbol of opposition to Russian encroachment and domination. The one significant achievement of the colony came in the field of language. This was the first translation of the New Testament into the Tatar-Turkish language, made by Henry Brunton and published in 1813.

Little is known of Brunton's early life. He came from Selkirk and had previously worked for the Edinburgh Missionary Society in West Africa between 1797 and 1800. Obviously a man of considerable linguistic ability, he had compiled there the first grammar of the Susu language, which was published in 1802. The Susu were Mohammedans and Brunton developed an interest in Arabic which was to help him in his work at Karass. His death, shortly before the publication of the New Testament, was a great loss to the colony.

The Reverend William Glen, a missionary at the Astrakhan station, wrote of Brunton, in his *Journal of a Tour from Astrachan to Karass* (1823), that he was '... a man of a most vigorous understanding, well skilled in the sacred literature of Europe, extensively acquainted with the dogmas of the Mohammedans, whose Coran he could read in the original Arabic; endowed with a singular capacity for acquiring a knowledge of dead and living languages, of a shrewd, active, enterprising turn of mind, and by consequence (in as far as natural capacity and extensive erudition are concerned) eminently qualified for the work of a Christian missionary'. Robert Lyall, a Scottish doctor who worked in Russia for several years, cited Glen's appraisal of Brunton in his *Travels in Russia, the Krimea, the Caucasus and Georgia* (1825), but could not forbear to add:

Mr Glen, in alluding to the failings of his brother-labourer, in the above parenthesis, did well to let the veil remain untouched, for it is ever to be regretted that it was the lot of a man of Brunton's talents to have been, as it were, expatriated and secluded from society. Perhaps consequent melancholy drove him to seek relief in liberal potations, which may have accelerated death.

Obviously Brunton developed a drink problem (which may have been connected with the death of his wife), but Lyall's comments are not completely clear, and he does not provide any sources for them though, presumably, he talked with people who had known Brunton.

However, Brunton did manage to complete his translation. The language of his New Testament was not, in fact, designed to be in the form of one particular Tatar dialect, but to form a medium between written literary Turkish and the various colloquial dialects of the surrounding Tatar tribes. 'A work that may be considered as a kind of standard or model for those who wish to write agreeably to the Turkish grammar, yet in such a style as to be understood by Tatars possessed of a moderate knowledge of their own language', was how the Reverend Glen appraised it.

Some of the same problems which hampered the work of the Karass colony were also met with by another group of missionaries, thousands of miles away to the east in Siberia. This was not a Scottish enterprise as such, though two Scots were part of the original four-man team sent out by the London Missionary Society in 1819 to establish a mission among the Buriat peoples of Siberia at the settlement of Selenginsk on the far side of Lake Baikal.

Two more Scots, John Paterson and Robert Pinkerton, played key roles in the planning of the mission. Pinkerton had been one of the early missionaries at Karass, before resigning through ill-health, though he later travelled extensively in Russia, on behalf of the British and Foreign Bible Society. Paterson, who was born at Duntochter, near Glasgow, in 1776, had preached for several years in Scandinavia before settling in St Petersburg. They were both closely involved with the founding, in 1812, of the Russian Bible Society. This Society, whose main task was the printing and distribution of Bibles and Scriptures throughout the Russian Empire, flourished during Alexander I's mystical and evangelical phase, but lost favour towards the end of his reign and was suspended by Nicholas I in 1826. Paterson had become printing and distribution manager for the Society in St Petersburg while Pinkerton had established a Moscow branch.

Both men (who, incidentally, seem to have cordially disliked each other) were instrumental in persuading the London Missionary Society to establish a mission in the Irkutsk region of Siberia. With Alexander on the throne government support was thought probable, while the projected site for the mission was considered suitably central for evangelizing among the heathen peoples of Siberia. However, it was erroneously believed that the proximity of the mission to the Chinese border would allow a future eventual penetration of that country. Also incorrect was the belief that a mastery of the Mongolian language of the Buriats would provide, through its closeness to the Manchu language, a linguistic key to China.

William Swan.

The mission itself lasted a little more than twenty years from 1819 until its closure in 1840. One of the original quartet of missionaries, the Swede Cornelius Rahm, had to return because of his wife's ill-health, leaving behind him the Englishman Edward Stallybrass and the Scots William Swan and Robert Yuille with their families. The small town of Selenginsk lay on the east bank of the river Selenga some 100 miles east of Lake Baikal, and the mission station was built on the opposite bank. Later, additional stations were established further to the north to help the missionaries travel more easily among the Buriat tribes.

However, as at Karass, the hoped-for mass conversions never took place. The Buddhism of the Buriats was not only a religious faith but a source of cultural strength and identity resistant to the missionaries' preachings. Moreover, the brand of Christianity they were attempting to propagate differed from the official creed of the Empire. There were thus no material advantages in converting as there might have been for native peoples in the British Empire. When the Russian Orthodox Church took up missionary activity in this area later in the century they made many thousands of converts, though it is difficult to know how many of them became genuine Christians.

Once again the missionaries' main achievement came in the field of language. William Swan (born at Milltown of Balgonie, near Leven, Fife, in 1791) and Edward Stallybrass completed between them the first translation of the whole Bible into Mongolian. R. C. Bawden, in his history of the Selenginsk mission describes the enormity of their task thus:

The Bible Society itself was less than twenty years old when they set to work, and there was little general experience in translating the Bible to go on. In preparation they had first of all to learn Russian and some Manchu, the contemporary keys to a mastery of Mongolian, the target language. They then had to analyse the Mongolian language and reduce it to order. They had to distinguish between the written language, with its archaic grammatical system and spelling and the spoken Buryat, which differed considerably from it, and to compile their own grammars and dictionaries. To do this with understanding they had to plough their way through hundreds of pages of uncongenial Mongolian literature, Buddhist sutras, cosmologies, legends, medical treatises, handbooks of divination and so on.

Bawden believes that, as pioneer scholars of Mongolian, they could have won themselves international reputations had they so wished. But, of course, they undertook their work of translation only as a means to an end, which, for reasons outside their control, was totally unrealizable.

As a postscript to the story of both missions we may

quote from an incident recounted by the historian and journalist D. Mackenzie Wallace, who was travelling through the Caucasus in the 1870s. He had noticed the name 'Shotlandskaia koloniia' on a map of the district he was in. His curiosity aroused, he visited the place itself but could obtain no information on any Scots living there until advised to consult an old man who lived at the end of the village. He then recalls:

…I found a venerable old man, with fine venerable features of the Circassian type, coal-black sparkling eyes, and a long grey beard that would have done honour to a patriarch. To him I explained briefly, in Russian, the object of my visit, and asked whether he knew any Scotsmen in the district.

'And why do you wish to know?' he replied, in the same language, fixing me with his keen, sparkling eyes.

'Because I am myself a Scotsman and hoped to find fellow-countrymen here.'

Let the reader imagine my astonishment when, in reply to this, he answered in genuine broad Scotch, 'Oh, man I'm a Scotsman tae! My name is John Abercrombie. Did you never hear tell o' John Abercrombie, the famous Edinburgh doctor?'

I was fairly puzzled by this extraordinary declaration. Dr Abercrombie's name was familiar to me as that of a medical practitioner and writer on psychology, but I knew that he was long since dead. When I had recovered a little from my surprise, I ventured to remark to the enigmatical personage before me that, though his tongue was certainly Scotch, his face was as certainly Circassian.

'Weel, weel,' he replied, evidently enjoying my look of mystification, 'you're no far wrang. I'm a Circassian Scotsman!'

It turned out that Abercrombie had been one of the children purchased by the Karass missionaries to be brought up as a Christian. As the money for his purchase had been subscribed by Dr John Abercrombie he had, on being baptised, taken the latter's name. Having learnt the trade of printing at Karass, he had worked for the missionaries at Selenginsk in that capacity for several years until the mission closed. Afterwards he had returned to the Caucasus and remained there as one of the last living relics of two heroically unsuccessful enterprises.

The monument at Selenginsk erected by Robert Yuille in memory of his wife, Martha.

SELECT BIBLIOGRAPHY

IA. A. Balagurov, *Olonetskie gornye zavody v doreformennyi period,* Petrozavodsk, 1958.

R. P. Bartlett, 'Charles Gascoigne in Russia', in *Russia and the West in the eighteenth century,* ed. A.G. Cross, Newtonville, Mass., 1983.

R. C. Bawden, *Shamans, lamas and evangelicals: the English missionaries in Siberia,* London, 1985.

R. H. Campbell, *Carron Company,* Edinburgh, 1961.

J. G. James, 'Russian iron bridges to 1850', *Transactions of the Newcomen Society,* 53 (1981-2), 79-104.

M. V. Jones, 'The sad and curious story of Karass', *Oxford Slavonic Papers,* N.S.8 (1975), 53-81.

E. Robinson, 'The transference of British technology to Russia, 1760-1820', in *Great Britain and her world, 1750-1914,* ed. by B. M. Ratcliffe, Manchester, 1975.

Russkii biograficheskii slovar', 25v. (New York, 1962; reprint of Moscow-St Petersburg ed. of 1896-1918).

T. Tower, *Memoir of the late Charles Baird, Esq., of St Petersburg, and of his son, the late Francis Baird, Esq., of St Petersburg and 4 Queens Gate,* London. London, 1867.

CALEDONIA AND RUS': SOME LITERARY CROSS-REFERENCES
IAN McGOWAN

RUSSIA, no less than the countries of Western Europe, if somewhat later than them, experienced the great literary movements that marked the end of the 18th and the beginning of the 19th centuries. Neo-Classicism, largely based on French models, was about to be superseded by Romanticism, looking towards Germany and Great Britain. The literature of feeling and the sublime would seek to oust the literature of reason and scepticism. At a mid point in this process, in the decades around the turn of the 18th century, the Russian Sentimental school flourished. Among the authors from whom they derived their inspiration, the names of James Thomson and Macpherson's Ossian are particularly prominent, and it is in this context that the first specifically Scottish influences on Russian literature can be seen.

Widely-known as Thomson was in Russia, he was not generally associated with Scotland as a separate national, geographical and cultural entity. The same can not be said of Ossian, whose name conjured up the image of a wild, melancholy and romantically beautiful land, swathed in mist, and populated by characters from Celtic, and sometimes, indiscriminately, Scandinavian folklore. These images captured the imagination of the Russians, as of the rest of Europe. In particular, the poems of Ossian fed the enthusiasm of the Sentimentalists, such as Karamzin, for the melancholy, and for the contemplation of departed glories, which for some critics demonstrated the affinity of Ossian's songs and the 'Russian soul'. Apart from a fragment in the Russian translation of Goethe's *Die Leiden des Jungen Werthers* (1781), the first translations of Ossian into Russian were by A. I. Dmitriev, and included in his *Poemy drevnikh bardov* (*Poems of the Ancient Bards*, 1788), and versions of 'Carthon' and 'Songs of Selma' by Karamzin (1791). The first complete translation was a version in prose by Kostrov from the French of Letourneur, and dedicated to General Suvorov, who was said to have taken the works of Ossian with him on his campaigns.

The success and influence of Ossian were immediate. Translations, imitations, and dramas continued to be produced until the 1830s. At the beginning of the century, Ossian's songs were used for prize recitations in schools 'because of their elevation of feeling and their novelty, but especially because of their quality of beauty of form, thought, and expression'. Ossianic images and names are found in Karamzin and Derzhavin, Zhukovskii and Pushkin, whose early poems include two, 'Kol'na' (1813) and 'Osgar' (1814), on Ossianic themes. The poet Lermontov had a particular cause for interest in all things Scottish, since his ancestor, George Learmonth, a Scot in the service of Poland, was captured by the Russians in 1613, and subsequently settled in Russia. In 1830 Lermontov wrote 'Grob Ossiana' ('The Grave of Ossian'), which describes the grave 'V gorakh Shotlandii moei' ('In the mountains of my Scotland'), and in the following year in 'Zhelanie' ('The Wish') he writes of the sea that separates him from Scotland, his native land.

As well as stimulating interest in Scotland, Ossian played a significant part in the growth of interest in Russia's own past, its preservation in folklore, and its representation in literature. Translators of Ossian turned to the metre and imagery of Russian folklore to convey the spirit of the original to this new audience, and in so doing helped to kindle the interest in the ancient literary heritage of Russia, a spark that burst into flame

Ossian, a lithograph of 1839 by N. I. Tonci, an Italian artist domiciled in Russia.

with the publication of the newly discovered *Slovo o polku Igoreve* (The song of Igor's host) in 1800. The 'Slovo', a 12th-century epic poem, the authenticity of which has been disputed periodically, was immediately compared by Karamzin to the 'beaux morceaux d'Ossian', thereby defining the context in which the Russian work should be understood. As the contemporary critic, IU. D. Levin, has written, 'the Scottish bard was a means of interpreting the Russian poet'.

The interest in Russia's past engendered by Ossian and Ossianism was complemented by the intense Russian patriotism stirred by the Napoleonic wars and the invasion of Russia by Napoleon in 1812. After his immense success with the drama *Fingal*, the dramatist V. A. Ozerov turned to native themes with *Dmitrii Donskoi*, celebrating the victory over the Golden Horde at Kulikovo in 1380. At the same time as he was writing 'Kol'na', the young Pushkin was also celebrating Russian feats of arms. Heroism and valour in battle, together with love of country, became the aspects of Ossianism most influential at this period. However, in the 1820s, the influence of Ossian on the major figures of Russian literature declined, as other writers, notably Sir Walter Scott, captured the attention of Pushkin and his contemporaries.

Scott reached probably the widest audience of any foreign author in Russia in the 19th century, and his influence can be seen not only in the development of the Russian historical novel, but also in the vogue for wearing tartan, 'Walter Scott' cloaks, and dressing up as characters from his novels. Russians were fascinated by Scott the man, as well as the author, and displayed as much interest in his domestic circumstances as in his work. Kozlov's poem 'K Val'ter Skottu' ('To Walter Scott'), for example, describes how he dreams of a visit to Abbotsford:

> Scottish bard, singer beloved
> of a beautiful, wild country...
> How often I, in joyful dreams,
> From gloomy and oppressive thoughts
> Fly to shady Abbotsford,
> I yearn to stay a while with you, my bard.

> Shotlandskii bard, pevets liubimyi
> Prekrasnoi dikoi storony...
> Kak chasto ia, v mechtakh veselykh,
> Ot myslei mrachnykh i tiazhelykh
> V tenistyi Abbotsford lechu,
> S toboi, moi bard, pozhit' khochu.

The poem paints an intimate picture of Scott surrounded by his grandchildren, telling tales of 'corpses, witches and fortune-tellers' and singing 'native ballads'. A number of Russians did manage to join what Lockhart called the 'staring worshippers from foreign parts', and visited Abbotsford in reality, where, judging by the account of his visit in 1828 written by A. I. Turgenev to his brother, the Decembrist and political émigré N. I. Turgenev, they were treated with great kindness and hospitality.

For some, contact with Scott was by correspondence. Scott was as eager for information about Russia for his life of Napoleon as Russians were for information about the great novelist, and his correspondents included Denis Davydov, known as the Black Captain, the partisan leader and hero of 1812. Scott had referred to the alliance of Great Britain and Russia against Napoleon in his welcoming verses addressed to the Grand Duke Nicholas in 1816:

> Hail! then, hail! illustrious stranger;
> Welcome to our mountain strand;
> Mutual interests, hopes, and danger,
> Link us with thy native land.
> Freemen's force, or false beguiling,
> Shall that union ne'er divide,
> Hand in hand while peace is smiling,
> And in battle side by side.

In 1828 Scott wrote to Davydov:

I am extremely desirous to know a little in detail the character of the partizan war conducted with so much adventure, spirit and indefatigable activity in the campaign of Moscow... a few sketches or anecdotes, however slight, from the hand of the Black Captain would be esteemed by me an inestimable favour.

I have been able to procure a drawing of Captain Davydov which hangs above one of the things I hold most precious, namely a good broadsword which was handed down to me by my ancestors.

Davydov was occupied by military campaigns in the Caucasus at this time, and the sketches and anecdotes were never sent. However, through Davydov's nephew, Vladimir Davydov, who was studying at Edinburgh and had visited Scott, the two men exchanged gifts, a portrait of Scott for Davydov and a sword and dagger from Davydov to join Scott's ancestral weaponry.

Scott opened wider the door through which Russia glimpsed the life, history and culture of Scotland, but his importance is equally measured by the influence he had on Russian literature. The period of Scott's greatest fame coincided with, and helped to determine, the rise of the novel as the most important genre in Russian literature. The critic Belinskii wrote:

Walter Scott has created, invented, discovered, or, still better, has divined the epic of our time—the historical novel. Many persons bearing the impress of great talent or even genius have followed in his train; yet he has remained a genius of a unique kind.

In the 1820s and 1830s the Russians responded enthusiastically to Scott's realistic descriptions of people, places and events, spiced with abundant local colour and imbued with an

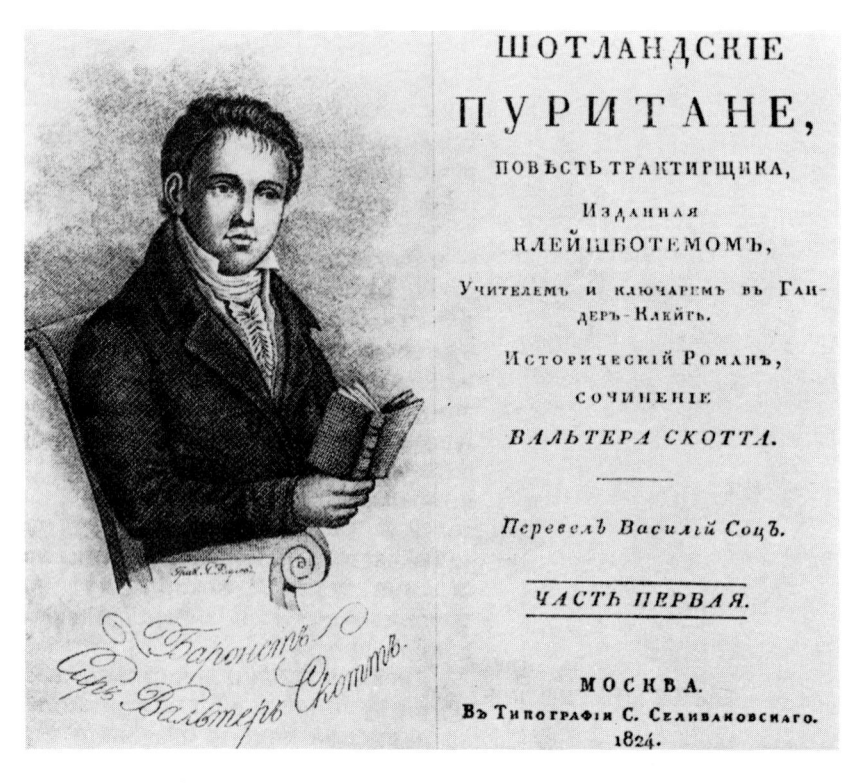

Title-page of an early Russian translation of *Tales of my Landlord*.

independent national spirit. Scott's works, originally read in French, and later translated into Russian from French versions, inspired a number of enormously popular historical novels, such as Zagoskin's *Iurii Miloslavskii* (published in London, in 1833, as *The Young Muscovite*), and Bestuzhev-Marlinskii's *Romantic Tales*, but the greatest of the writers to be touched by Scott was undoubtedly Alexander Pushkin. Of the three great influences on Pushkin from European literature, Byron, Shakespeare and Scott, the influence of Scott is most marked in Pushkin's prose, particularly the historical fiction, but is not confined to it.

It is clear from the draft of a letter to the poet and translator Gnedich, written when Pushkin was twenty-two, that he expected Byron and Scott to be the standards by which his own poem, 'Kavkazskii plennik' ('A Prisoner of the Caucasus') would be judged:

The local colour is accurate, but will it prove pleasing to readers pampered by the poetic panoramas of Byron and Walter Scott? I am even afraid of bringing them to mind by my pale, feeble sketches—the comparison will prove fatal to me.

Most of Scott's poetic works were known to Pushkin, either from the original or from French translations, and many of them were in his library. In 1828 he wrote 'Voron k voronu letit', a paraphrase of 'The Twa Corbies' from *The Minstrelsy of the Scottish Border*, but using a metre common in Russian folk poetry, and including elements from Russian folklore.

In 1824 Pushkin was living in virtual exile at his parents' estate in Mikhailovskoe, and among the comforts he asked his brother to send from St Petersburg were wine, rum, Limburg cheese and 'the new Walter Scott', which he calls 'food for the soul'. This spiritual nourishment fed Pushkin's growing interest in the possibilities of using Russian history as the subject of a new kind of prose. He wrote:

The chief fascination of Walter Scott's novels lies in the fact that we grow acquainted with the past, not encumbered with the *enflure* of French tragedies, or with the prudery of the novels of sentiment, or with the *dignité* of history, but in a contemporary, homely manner.

Pushkin's interest in historical writing eventually led him to choose as the subject of an historical novel the rebellion of Pugachev during the reign of Catherine II. He visited places associated with Pugachev, collected material locally and in the state archives, although deteriorating relations with Tsar Nicholas I made it more and more difficult to gather original material. At the same time he continued to read Scott avidly, and the resulting work, *Kapitanskaia dochka* (*The Captain's Daughter*), follows Scott in setting a fictitious family chronicle against a background of historical events, presented realistically with abundant local colour.

The influence of Scott was felt, of course, by other Russian writers of the period as well as by Pushkin. Translations and adaptations of Scott's verse were produced by Kozlov and Zhukovskii, both of whom knew Scott in the original. A. A. Shakhovskoi began to adapt Scott's works for the stage at the beginning of the 1820s, and the great success of plays such as 'Ivanhoe' (1822) contributed a great deal to Scott's wider popularity. What Viazemskii, the poet and friend of Pushkin, called the 'fever of curiosity, yearning, avidity, and enthusiasm' excited by Scott gave impetus to the particular development of Russian prose and paved the way for the eventual appearance of the classic novels of the 19th-century Russian tradition.

In contrast to the fame that Sir Walter Scott enjoyed in Russia during his life, Robert Burns's achievements took longer to be recognized, and he became widely known in Russia only after his death. His 'Address To the Shade of Thomson' was translated in 1800, although it seems that Thomson was of greater significance to the translator than was Burns. It was not until the 1820s that Burns's name began to appear in Russian reviews of foreign literature, such as Sreznevskii's 'Opyt kratkoi poetiki' ('Brief essay in poetics', 1821), and only achieved a measure of fame after the publication in 1829 of a version of 'The Cotter's Saturday Night' ('Sel'skii subottnii vecher v Shotlandii: vol'noe podrazhenie R. Burnsu'—'A rural Saturday Evening in Scotland: a free imitation of R. Burns'), by the blind Romantic poet, Ivan Kozlov. To Burns's verses Kozlov adds an apostrophe to Russia, comparing Burns's love of his homeland with his own feelings for Russia:

> O, how dear is Scotland to the poet!…
>
> But I appeal to you, to you,
> Holy Rus', our mother-land!
> Flourish, flourish, my native country!
>
> O, kak pevtsu Shotlandiia mila!…
> A ia k tebe, k tebe vzyvaiu ia,
> Sviataia Rus', o nasha mat'-zemlia!
> Tsveti, tsveti, strana moia rodnaia!

This work of Kozlov led to the first article devoted to Burns to be published in Russia, Nikolai Polevoi's 'O zhizni i sochineniiakh R. Bornsa' ('On the Life and Works of R. Burns'). Polevoi emphasized particularly the proof provided by Burns that poetic genius is as likely to be found in the humbly-born as in the nobility, and that greatness does not depend on circumstances of birth or wealth. From this time, any poet of lowly origins was liable to be called 'the Russian Burns'.

While there were many mediocre translations and imitations of Burns in the 1830s and 1840s, the first translations of literary worth were those by Mikhail Mikhailov published in Nekrasov's famous journal *Sovremennik* in 1856. Burns was now firmly established as a standard-bearer for the progressive camp which dominated Russian literature in the 1860s, and was translated by a number of poets associated with the revolutionary movement. They tended to emphasize the civic elements in Burns at the expense of the more personal, but it was largely by these translations that Burns was known until the present century. That Russian interest in Burns has grown ever greater since the Revolution is due mainly to the translations of Tatiana Shchepkina-Kupernik and Samuil Marshak. The translations of Marshak especially have ensured that Burns is as familiar to Russians as many native poets, and that there is a permanent place for Burns within Russian literature.

Marshak, who studied in England before the First World War and began translating from English poetry at that time, turned his attention to Burns in 1924 and continued to produce translations of Burns until his death in 1964. IU. D. Levin gives a modern Soviet view of his work:

Manuscript of Marshak's translation of Burns's 'The Guidwife of Wauchope-House'.

Marshak's translations are far from being accurate in the literal sense. One can discover divergences between them and the originals—these are altogether unavoidable in verse translations, especially from English into Russian—virtually in every line. But close analysis shows that these frequent deviations make possible the re-creation, in accordance with the rules of Russian, of the totality of a poem: Marshak reconstitutes not merely its verbal content but also the style, the imagery, the emotional tone, its simplicity and its dramatic quality, its dynamic and its musicality—in short, he renders all the features whereby the translation acquires the charm and magic of the original.

Emrys Hughes, MP for South Ayrshire from 1946 to his death in 1969 and a personal friend of Marshak, was present at Marshak's funeral, and later wrote a moving account of it that included this summary of his achievement:

He did for Burns in Russian what Edward Fitzgerald did for us in Omar Khayaam, but much more so for his translations of Burns ran into two volumes and he was still translating them when he died. He had introduced millions of Russians to Tam o' Shanter and Souter Johnnie, to John Anderson and Holy Willie and the Jolly Beggars and taught them to sing 'Comin' through the Rye' and 'Auld Lang Syne' and to recite 'A man's a man for a' that'.

So it was fitting that among the medals that lay beside his coffin were not only the Order of Lenin but his much treasured badge of the Honorary President of the Burns Federation which had come from Scotland.

Another aspect of the impact of Scottish literary life on Russian culture is demonstrated by the part played in the development of modern Russian literature by the literary journal, represented today by journals such as *Novyi mir*, which have seen the appearance of some of the most significant works of Russian literature in their pages. There are frequent references in Pushkin's letters to the need for a Russian literary journal, to provide a forum for contemporary writers to publish their work and for the discussion of literary and other topics, and the model cited for such a journal is the *Edinburgh Review*.

As early as 1825, Pushkin wrote to Viazemskii, 'I get all the other reviews—and more than ever feel the need of something in the nature of the *Edinburgh Review*'. However, it was only in the last year of his life that the necessary permission was given to publish such a journal, *Sovremennik (The Contemporary)*, which, in spite of a ban on any overtly political content and an initially cool reception from the public, survived to become one of the most important vehicles for Russian literature in the 19th century.

While the *Edinburgh Review* inspired Pushkin to create a comparable Russian journal, and thereby played a part in the development of Russian literature in its native land, one of the earliest vehicles for making Russian literature more widely known in Britain was *Blackwood's Edinburgh Magazine* through its publication of the translations and articles of Thomas Budge Shaw (1813-1862). After graduating from Trinity College, Cambridge, and acting as a private tutor, Shaw settled in Russia in 1841, becoming Assistant Professor of English literature at the Imperial Lyceum in Tsarskoe Selo, and subsequently Lecturer in English Language at St Petersburg University, and tutor to the Grand Dukes of Russia, including the future Tsar Alexander III.

In 1843 *Blackwood's* published Shaw's translation of Bestuzhev-Marlinskii's *Amalat Bek*, rightly described in the translator's Preface as 'the first attempt to introduce to the British public any work of Russian Prose Fiction whatever, with anything like a reasonable selection of subject and character, at least *directly* from the original language'. In a letter to John Blackwood in March 1843, Shaw described *Blackwood's Edinburgh Magazine* as 'the only English publication of its kind at all extensively known or read in Russia', and outlined his plans for more translations and critical articles, including a biography of Pushkin. Shaw's motives in submitting his work to *Blackwood's* were at least partly financial. He had started to publish a journal in English in St Petersburg, only to discover, as many before and since, the precarious economics of such an enterprise, described in a letter of September 1844 as 'a truly deplorable speculation, which has gone to a hundred and sixty three cartloads of devils, and went out like a sky rocket, leaving me with very smart liabilities'.

BLACKWOOD'S
EDINBURGH MAGAZINE.

No. CCCXXIX.　　　MARCH, 1843.　　　Vol. LIII.

AMMALÁT BEK.

A TRUE TALE OF THE CAUCASUS.

TRANSLATED FROM THE RUSSIAN OF MARLÍNSKI. BY THOMAS B. SHAW, B.A. OF CAMBRIDGE, ADJUNCT PROFESSOR OF ENGLISH LITERATURE IN THE IMPERIAL LYCEUM OF TSARSKOË SELO.

THE TRANSLATOR'S PREFACE.

THE English mania for travelling, which supplies our continental neighbours with such abundant matter for wonderment and witticism, is of no very recent date. Now more than ever, perhaps, does this passion seem to possess us:

"——— tenet insanabile multos
Tartarum κακοήθες, et ægro in corde senescit:"

when the press groans with "Tours," "Trips," "Hand-books," "Journeys," "Visits."

In spite of this, it is as notorious as unaccountable, that England knows very little, or at least very little correctly, of the social condition, manners, and literature of one of the most powerful among her continental sisters.

The friendly relations between Great Britain and Russia, established in the reign of Edward V., have subsisted without interruption since that epoch, so auspicious to both nations: the bond of amity, first knit by Chancellor in 1554, has never since been relaxed: the two nations have advanced, each at its own pace, and by its own paths, towards the sublime goal of improvement and civilization—have stood shoulder to shoulder in the battle for the weal and liberty of mankind.

It is, nevertheless, as strange as true, that the land of Alfred and Elizabeth is yet but imperfectly acquainted with the country of Peter and of Catharine. The cause of this ignorance is assuredly not to be found in any indifference or want of curiosity on the part of English travellers. There is no lack of pilgrims annually leaving the bank of Thames,

"With cockle hat and staff,
With gourd and sandal shoon;"

armed duly with note-book and "patent Mordan," directing their wandering steps to the shores of Ingria, or the gilded cupolas of Moscow. But a very

Preface to Shaw's translation of *Ammalat Bek*.

Shaw's relationship with *Blackwood's* was more stable and, in spite of the difficulties of transmitting his work to Edinburgh in winter with Baltic navigation closed, allowed him to recover his financial position, and to publish in 1845 the first significant articles on Pushkin to appear in English, together with what he described as 'Daguerrotypes from Russian poetry', as well as a separately published translation of Lazhechnikov's *The Heretic (Basurman)*, and in 1847 Gogol's *The Portrait (Portret)*. *Blackwood's Edinburgh Magazine* has, therefore, an honourable place among the pioneers who laid the foundations for an appreciation of Russian literature in the West, and created the conditions in which a trickle of translations from a still little-known literature became within fifty years a flood.

SELECT BIBLIOGRAPHY

M. P. Alekseev, *Russko-angliiskie literaturnye sviazi (XVIII vek-pervaia polovina XIX veka)*, Literaturnoe nasledstvo 91, Moscow, 1982.

M. Green, 'Some aspects of Scottish authors in Russian literature in the first half of the nineteenth century', unpublished Ph.D. thesis, University of Edinburgh, 1955.

IU. D. Levin, 'Russian Responses to the Poetry of Ossian', in *Great Britain and Russia in the Eighteenth Century*, edited by A. G. Cross, Newtonville, Mass., 1979), 47-64.

IU. D. Levin, 'The Russian Burns. The Reception of Robert Burns in Pre-revolutionary and Soviet Times', *Scottish Slavonic Review*, 5 (1985), 36-71.

M. B. Line, *A bibliography of Russian literature in English translation to 1900 (excluding periodicals)*, London, 1963.

V. I. Maslov, *Ossian v Rossii (bibliografiia)*, Leningrad, 1928.

Pushkin on literature, edited by Tatiana Wolff, revised edition, London, 1986.

E. J. Simmons, *English literature and culture in Russia (1553-1840)*, Cambridge, Mass., 1935.

G. Struve, 'A Russian Traveller in Scotland in 1828: Alexander Turgenev', *Blackwood's Magazine*, 258, (November 1945), 342-349.

G. Struve, 'Russian friends and Correspondents of Sir Walter Scott', *Comparative Literature*, 2, no. 4 (Fall 1950), 307-326.

Jessie Carrick (née Lauder).

Andrew Carrick

THE CARRICKS OF ST PETERSBURG

FELICITY ASHBEE

ONE of my early memories as a small child is walking slowly down the big staircase in my grandmother's house looking up at the family portraits. There was room for quite a few of them, for the staircase, generously planned when the house was built in 1880, had plenty of wall-space. From their heavy gold frames our Scottish ancestors looked down at us.

Most splendid of them was my great grandmother Jessie Carrick, née Lauder, who seemed to lean almost voluptuously out of her frame, a little jewel on a narrow band on her forehead setting off her gleaming ringlets. Her gown was off the shoulders, and big bouffant sleeves of some transparent material added to the glamorous image. Her husband Andrew hung next to her, but though the painter had given him a slightly Byronic cloak and red cravat, and a lowering sky and fragment of Scottish mountain behind him, he did not inspire quite the same romantic feeling.

Above these two paintings hung two Lauder Aunts, I don't even remember ever being told their names. They were probably maiden aunts, living somewhat restricted lives as poor relations or extra helpers with the family. Both wore severe dark dresses and shawls, and had little white frilled caps framing serious faces. Below these large portraits, and better lit by the bluish, hairbell-shaped lamp at the stairhead, were four far more interesting pictures. More interesting to us children, at least, because they were of children. Two were schoolboys, probably aged about twelve and ten, the tougher held a cricket bat, the more sensitive had a water-colour paint-box at his elbow. They were Great-Uncle Edward Forbes, and his younger brother Grandpapa Francis Forbes.

But next to them were the two pictures we liked the best. They were of a little boy and girl, he about six, she four years old. They were George Lyon Carrick and his little sister Jessie-Mary, the two younger children of the romantic Jessie and her husband. They were born in Kronshtadt, the port of St Petersburg, where the family had settled with their eldest son William in 1828. This first child had been born on the last day of 1827, and been taken with them to Russia as a baby in arms. The Russian artist who painted the portraits of George and little Jessie left no clue to his identity, but the story went that she had been reluctant to be called in from play for her sitting. As a result her dimpled face wore a look of sulky boredom; even the line of her small sloping shoulders, left bare by the low white frock with its blue satin bows, emphasized the mood.

By contrast, an irrepressible George, in blue velvet and a cloud of curls, looked out at the world open-heartedly, giving perhaps a hint already of the charming, good-natured, amusing spendthrift he was to become. They were all dead, we knew, except for Great-Uncle Edward, who, stone deaf, and with a Father Christmas beard, held sway over a stately Gothic residence near Godstone, and Jessie-Mary—'Babushka'—(the Russian for Grandmother), as she always insisted on being called. We found it hard to believe as we reached up to be kissed by this old, old lady with her snowy curls, and boned net collar above the black dress ridged with tiny tucks, and bedangled with gold chains and jet ornaments, that this could possibly be the sulky little beauty hanging in the shadows on the stairs. It was just as hard, too, to realize that the boy with the paintbox, after a ten-year courtship by post, had actually made her his bride!

The Carrick family was not unique. The world is full of descendants of Scots who left their native land to seek their fortunes in countries which offered them greater opportunities for their talent and initiative. Andrew Carrick's father, also William, is described in the family tree as early as 1783, as 'Merchant of St Petersburg', but it is not known where Andrew himself was born. He does not appear to have been registered in 1802 in either the British church records in St Petersburg, or in Edinburgh. Perhaps, wherever they were living, they were not church-goers. But the younger William had been christened in Edinburgh before his parents took him to Russia, and both George and Jessie-Mary's christenings are recorded in the register of the British Community in Kronshtadt.

Andrew Carrick's business flourished. His young wife, whom he had married before her seventeenth birthday, proved to be not only statuesquely good-looking, but an original, warm-hearted and spontaneous being who adapted easily to Russian ways. Their circle expanded and began to include not only business contacts, and wealthy owners of estates, whose forests Andrew would have to visit to make contracts for the standing timber, but also artists and musicians. One of their closer friends was the Polish artist, a Gold Medal winner at the St Petersburg Academy of Arts, Xavier Jan Kaniewski, who, in 1833, did an elegant water-colour miniature of Andrew, followed the same year by the two big oil portraits now hanging on our stairs. So when it became clear in 1844, that the sixteen-year-old William was beginning to show greater aptitude for art than for business, it was natural that Kaniewski's advice should be sought. With his help, and perhaps that of others with influence in the Carricks' circle, William got all the right introductions, and in the spring of 1844 entered the Academy of Arts as a student in the Architectural Department. He was already startlingly good-looking. Six foot four in his stocking-feet, with luxuriant black hair and grey-blue eyes. At the same time he had a charming disposition, a sense of humour, and a beautiful singing voice. These combined attributes made him a welcome guest in many St Petersburg homes.

Jessie-Mary, George and William Carrick with their mother.

But architecture did not inspire him, and he moved from department to department trying to find what he really enjoyed doing most. Finally he settled for water-colour portraits, and after studying for the unusually long period of nine years, he passed his examinations, and, his parents being willing and the business able to finance him, he went, as most other artist-graduates from Russia did, for further study to 'the Artists' Paradise'—Rome. Here he spent another three years, from 1853-1856, during the last two years of which, the Crimean War was being waged. Though this does not seem to have affected the life of the international artistic community in Rome, it had a very serious effect on the timber trade between Britain and Russia, for Canadian forests began to displace the hitherto largely exclusive Russian sources. When William finally returned to St Petersburg, he found his father a very worried man.

But something else had almost certainly happened to William while he was in Rome. He had become fascinated by the idea of photography as the 'art form' of the future. Faced with the task of having to earn his own living, he broke the news to his parents that he was going to abandon the old art for the new one. It was a very disturbing moment for artists everywhere, for until the advent of 'the black box' they alone had been the arbiters of truth—of whether a portrait was a 'true' likeness, or whether nature was being 'truthfully' portrayed. Now everything could be compared with a photograph which seemed to offer the ultimate in truth. And not only artists were being judged by new standards. As photographs of artists' work began to appear, the engravers saw their means of livelihood vanishing almost overnight. But for those who had decided to take the plunge into photography, it was a very exciting moment.

William had studied in Rome at the same time as one Hoch (the Carrick and Hoch families were close friends in earlier days), and Hoch, who returned to St Petersburg a little earlier than William, must have decided to switch to photography at once. As soon as William had made the same decision, he began as a 'learner-assistant' in Hoch's studio. But this startling change of course was not the only topic of discussion that year amongst the members of the Carrick family. The Carrick's younger son George, now sixteen, had set his heart on becoming a doctor, and pursuing his medical studies in Scotland. In spite of the state of the business, there seems to have been no question of denying him this opportunity; at the same time, an even more difficult decision—for Mrs Carrick at least—was taken. To send fourteen-year-old Jessie to Edinburgh for a couple of years, for some good Scots discipline in a girls' boarding school!

By the summer of 1857 everything was arranged. Mrs Carrick, who had not visited the land of her birth for 29 years, felt that this was a unique opportunity to show off her family to her relatives, and at the same time make sure that both George and Jessie were satisfactorily installed in their respective establishments of learning. And what more natural than that William should accompany them. He, of course, jumped at the chance, since it would enable him to see what was happening in the world of photography in Scotland, to get some up-to-date information about equipment, and perhaps even to do some training with Scottish experts. And things went well, William became a student with the already established photographer James G. Tunney, and perhaps even more important, made friends with a photographic technician John Macgregor, whom he fired with the idea of joining him in St Petersburg to set up a photographic atelier as soon as he, William, could find suitable premises. George, meanwhile, was safely, if slightly reluctantly, housed with a doctor's family (he managed to transfer himself into lodgings on his own the following year!), and Jessie started her studies at the Scottish Institution, 20 Ainslie Place, under the strict but not unfriendly supervision of the two Principals, the Misses Haswell and Prynne.

Early that autumn Mrs Carrick and William returned to St Petersburg, sailing from Hull on 5 October 1857. They had a terrifying passage—'…waves mountains high'—Mrs Carrick wrote to Jessie as soon as she got back—'and the State rooms full of water…'. She would have been even more terrified had she known that William had been burning his Aunt Isabella's midnight oil reading Herzen's 'revolutionary' periodical *The*

Bell, which had appeared for the first time in London that June, and that, almost certainly, the first three numbers were in his baggage to share with friends on his return. It is hard to know if this was naiveté or daring on William's part, for what happened could have landed him in real trouble. He gave the three copies to an old friend from Art school days, called Zakharov, who handed them on to another, who in turn gave them to a third. This last rashly arranged a reading in a local tavern.[1] They were of course arrested! Under police questioning Zakharov admitted having received the journals from William, who was at once summoned to the famed Third Department (The Secret Police), where he was seen by a Prince Dolgorukov. The Tzarist Archive merely notes that the meeting took place, but what was said was not 'minuted'. William was probably told that because he was not a Russian citizen, it did not mean he could flout the laws of his adopted country with impunity. There seem to have been no further repercussions.

The following spring the family was overtaken by a real crisis: Andrew Carrick fell ill. It seems to have been a sudden attack which heralded some disease of the nervous system from which he never recovered. He slowly deteriorated. In an attempt to find some treatment, George wrote from Scotland that the Ben Rhydding Hydro in Yorkshire had an excellent reputation, and that if there was enough money, perhaps his mother could bring his ailing father over for a cure; this, in fact, was arranged in the summer of 1858. Mrs Carrick's sad plight so much moved Dr and Mrs Macleod who were in charge of the Hydro, that they suggested both George and Jessie should come for a fortnight of their summer holiday, free of charge, if they did not mind sharing their parents' beds. There was a tearfully happy reunion, George found himself another medical student to hobnob with, and Jessie, now just sixteen, made the acquaintance of this student's charge, the youngest patient at the Hydro, fourteen-year-old Frank Forbes, who was there alone for his asthma. It was this boy, with whom she audaciously initiated a correspondence on her return to her boarding school, who, ten years later, was to become her husband.

Meanwhile back in Kronshtadt, William wrestled with the business debts, and when he could snatch the time, roamed St Petersburg, hunting for somewhere to set up his studio. The following spring he at last found a suitable place, at no. 19 Malaia Morskaia, at the top end of the Nevsky Prospect, not far from St Isaac's Cathedral. He at once summoned John Macgregor, who lost no time in settling his affairs—he was a man almost without ties, his only brother having emigrated to America. Macgregor set sail for Russia in June 1859, and on his arrival the two friends at once set to work making a glassroom and getting the place ready to open. But Andrew Carrick's health had not been helped by the Yorkshire treatment. He continued to deteriorate and died in June 1860. However, in spite of this family tragedy and the huge difficulties posed by the still outstanding timber business debts, the initial expenses of setting up the photographic business and of finding the fees for George's medical training in Scotland, a chronic problem, William and Macgregor carried on and the first customers began to come for their portraits. Mrs Carrick was soon writing to George: '...I wish you saw little Macgregor now, the proud step and high head he carries when he is busy. I do not believe there were ever two souls born to live in such unity and concord together...' Mr Macgregor rapidly became one of the family, and Mrs Carrick soon decided to make good his neglected education. 'Mr Olger... is now giving Mac English lessons, and I believe he will soon be a perfect scholar. I am going to teach him French—the Russian he may pick up the best way he can...'. She also wrote about the first clients in the atelier, and the succession of often drunken peasants who were the only available material to be groomed into receptionists and darkroom assistants. In general, however, an atmosphere of enthusiastic optimism prevailed, and there was not '... one shade or cloud of misunderstanding amongst them.... There is is not a day passes without some new plan or future scheme being spoken of...'

A couple of years later William himself described the scene in the glassroom where he reigned supreme at least as far as the artistic posing of his subjects was concerned. In all technical matters 'Mr Mac', of course, had the last word. '...Princes and Princesses, Counts and Countesses, Generals

William Carrick in his studio.

and Corporals with their ladies, including flunkeys, chambermaids and scullions; all come up to our attic and sit for their likeness by turns. Come first served first; all alike, amiable and willing to do my best to please them. If I ever do make any difference, it is certainly towards the humbler and poorer class of customer. I pay more attention to them for they require it more than the loftier or richer. The days are now splendid, and it is with great pleasure that the posing and photographic process is gone through, whereas in dull weather, every drop of collodion bath and developing solution were grudged, knowing that no superior knowledge could increase the quality of a negative when deprived of light...'

After Andrew Carrick's death the family consisted of Mrs Carrick and Jessie, who had come back from her Edinburgh boarding school at the end of the summer term in 1859, and William and Macgregor, though the latter lived mainly in the studio, where William often stayed with him overnight. George was still in Scotland. The family's financially straightened circumstances do not seem to have prevented Mrs Carrick and Jessie from accepting invitations to the homes of most of their old friends, both the artistic and the business ones, which they had frequented in happier times. Mrs Carrick did occasionally complain of having to 'turn' a frock, or add new trimming to an old cap to conceal a lack of modernity, and it was sometimes even hard to find small change to pay the humble izvozchik to take them home after a party, but obviously both Mrs Carrick and her children were always welcome, and Jessie, like her brother William, had the asset of an attractive singing voice.

Jessie herself might well have found the days drag after the structured activity of the Scottish Institution, but on her return she told her mother all about her budding correspondence with the young Frank Forbes, and Mrs Carrick, after perhaps a passing thought that her impulsive daughter had been a little indiscreet, decided that there was safety in distance, and that with time on her hands, writing letters in both English and French could not but broaden the mind. Frank, though still only fifteen, was now studying in Geneva with his brother Edward, older than himself by just two years. When Edward left for home to enter the family stock-broking business, Frank had more time to himself, and the correspondence with Jessie became more regular, and—partly because it was now frequently in French—more amorous, even though the convention of calling each other brother and sister was still observed.

Not long after Frank in his turn came back to London to join his father and brother in the business, Mrs Forbes and Mrs Carrick began corresponding direct, and by 1863, Jessie and her mother were all set to go over on a visit to Kent. In fact it had been planned for the year before, but William could not get enough money together to pay for fares and several months' living expenses for both mother and sister. But at last in the summer of 1863 the great journey took place, and when the two young people met again after an interval of five years, the inevitable happened and they fell properly in love, and soon declared their passion to their respective parents. The reaction was unexpected and shattering, at least as far as Frank's father was concerned. Mr Forbes could think of no one more charming to have as a daughter-in-law than Jessie, but his son was too young at nineteen, and neither mature enough to take on the responsibilities of a wife, nor advanced enough in his business career to be able to afford one. If the young couple were prepared to wait five years for his blessing....

Meanwhile, of course, Mrs Carrick and Jessie could no longer decently remain under the Forbes's roof. Decorum decreed that they had to leave, and they hurriedly retreated to the relatives in Scotland. It took several months of letter-writing between Mrs Carrick, William and Macgregor, Mrs Forbes (who was sentimentally on the young lovers' side) with Mr Forbes joining in, and finally some anguished letters between Frank and Jessie, before a stage of understanding was reached enabling the young couple to meet again. They agreed to wait, though Mr Forbes insisted that Jessie must consider herself absolutely free. Mother and daughter sailed back to St Petersburg in the summer of 1864, and the correspondence between Jessie and Frank was resumed.

George, by this time, had nearly completed his medical training by gaining experience in the hospital in Leith, followed by a year at the Brompton Hospital for Diseases of the Chest in London. He came back to St Petersburg in 1865 to William and Macgregor's great relief, and was soon collecting some quite important patients, amongst them the composer Mussorgsky. He had both good looks and the prestige of a Scots medical degree, and it was not long before he was on the British Embassy list of doctors later figuring in Baedeker. That summer of 1865 Frank Forbes, to his mother's great trepidation, although he was now 'of age', insisted on visiting the Carricks in St Petersburg, George having assured the Forbes that the cholera was not bad that year! Jessie was thus at last able to show her fiancé the land of her birth, and to show him off to the friends of the family. And Frank, though still beardless, which made him look unfortunately young, was otherwise very presentable, and unlike other visitors from Britain, could at least speak excellent French. The relationship was truly cemented, and the lovers resigned themselves to a further three years' wait.

During this and the preceding year the photographic business at the Malaia Morskaia had been progressing steadily. William and Macgregor between them were developing three distinct areas of work. First, there was ordinary portrait photography, the stock-in-trade of the 'new Art'; then William's continued close connexion with his artist friends from his Academy of Art days, and a new friendship with the Court Painter, the Hungarian Zichy, led to the more active promotion of the idea of photographing works of art for reproduction purposes. Before the coming of the camera, the only way the average citizen could know of a painting or sculpture was by standing in front of the object itself, or by learning about it from an often inferior engraving. Now the camera could show works of art, if not yet in colour, at least in all the delicate tonal values of a sepia print. William must in many cases have taken his heavy equipment into his artist-friends' studios, for much of the work that he reproduced was too large or too heavy to be brought up into the top-floor glassroom of no. 19 Malaia Morskaia.

But gradually it was the third field that became the two friends' greatest interest: the recording of the life and work of the ordinary Russian people, the street salesmen of every kind of commodity, artisans, sweeps, knife-grinders, woodmen, postmen and milkgirls, the removal men and the icemen who delivered the great chunks of ice hacked from the frozen Neva to go into the cellars of every house in the city. At first, William simply brought them into the glassroom, but as his and Macgregor's skill increased, they went out first into their own backyard, then onto the streets, and into the markets of the capital, and finally further afield to take pictures of the peasants working in the fields and woods. The first ones he called his 'rasnoshchiki' or hawkers, or more generally his 'Russian Types', and Mrs Carrick's attitude to this unconventional interest of her beloved first-born was perforce changed when the Heir Apparent, to whom William had sent a set of 80 of these 'Types' in 1862, had been so impressed by them that he had presented William with a '...diamond ring, worth forty pounds... as a token of his appreciation...'

But the problem for the photography business was eternally one of lack of ready cash. William was constantly

Two of William Carrick's Russian types: a knife-grinder and a hawker of tools.

thwarted even when he got good orders for prints, by not having enough money to get materials, whether of developing solutions or Bristol boards for mounting; and he had also to keep his mother and sister in a reasonably contented state as regards their living standards and ability to 'go into society'. George, too, was frequently known to sit at the bedside of dying members of poorer patients' families, and then not have the heart to send in a bill. He was also not always diplomatic enough to keep his wealthier patients contented. His mother once complained with some justice, of how one of the Princes on George's list would demand his attendance at midnight after his and the Princess's return from the theatre. They could not be that ill, Mrs Carrick remarked, if they were well enough to go to the French play! George was also continuing his researches into possible cures for tuberculosis, the scourge of the times, and here his titled patients often helped; also his Brompton Hospital experience gave him kudos when discussing such matters with the more senior members of the profession in Russia.

In 1867 Frank Forbes came over on another visit to the Carricks, to finalise the plans for his and Jessie's wedding in St Petersburg. It was settled for the following summer. But one more crisis almost caused a last minute catastrophe. William had not succeeded in quite settling all the old timber business debts. Now one of the oldest creditors, previously a close friend of the family but one who had ceased to know them once Andrew had got into difficulties, suddenly demanded full payment. William landed up in the debtors' prison, and there was consternation in case this news should somehow leak out and become known to Jessie's future 'in-laws', thus spoiling all chance of the young couple's marriage and future happiness. Jessie and the distraught Mrs Carrick took refuge with discreet friends in the country, while George and 'Mr Mac' pulled every available string to get William out and the creditor paid off.

The wedding finally took place on 8 June 1868, Frank's brother Edward came over with him to be best man, and William gave his sister away. It was a quiet ceremony in the first floor chapel of the 'British Factory', an 1814 Quarenghi building on the English Quay. Over the Palladian columns at the altar end ran the words in gilded Roman lettering: THE SAME YESTERDAY, TODAY AND FOREVER. The words are still there today, though the building now serves another purpose. There was a simple reception at the Carrick's current home not far away in the Moshkov Pereulok, the guests walking home afterwards in the pale splendour of the White Nights. Frank took Jessie for a honeymoon to Switzerland on the way back to their new life together in England.

From then on the 'steam-packet' which used to carry Frank's and Jessie's love-letters between Kent and St Petersburg now took Mrs Carrick's weekly four pages of family and local news to her absent daughter. And William and Macgregor redoubled their efforts so that Mrs Carrick could visit her 'darling Jessie' for two or three months every summer until her death in 1876.

In 1871 William and Macgregor made their first really big expedition to the interior, to the Volga country of the Simbirsk province, the 'heartland' of Russia. Here they spent a whole month with a land-owner friend of William's, one Nicholai Sokovnin, an original character of liberal tendencies. Sokovnin's description of this visit is quoted in the memorial speech read to the Imperial Russian Technical Society a week after William's death.[2]

'He came to us in the Simbirsk Province with his colleague Macgregor, another simple, uncommercially minded soul like himself... They worked tirelessly, without resting, from sunrise to sunset, often producing up to 25 negatives a day, thus building up the marvellous collection of Great-Russian types and views, and of non-Russians, Mordovians, Chuvashes which we have seen in Carrick's portfolios. We went round in a big group together, covering a wide area, opening up new horizons, and racing to choose themes for yet more photographs ... Carrick's stay of a month with us went by as if it had been a day, and there cannot be a Mordovian, however cowed and humbled by fate, who appeared on one of his photographs, who would not even today grin when remembering him...'

But in 1872 a major tragedy overtook William and the business at the Malaia Morskaia. While his mother was stay-

Wood-scene in Simbirsk province, by William Carrick.

At Kamenka Fair, Simbirsk province, by William Carrick.

ing with Jessie and Frank in England, Macgregor suddenly died, after a short and unexplained illness. It left William rudderless and near to despair, their partnership having been one where the functions of each were clearly defined, yet perfectly attuned. Mrs Carrick hurried back to St Petersburg, but it was only some eight months later that William in his loneliness, finally brought himself to tell her that he had been secretly married for the last five years, though he had probably been attached to 'Sashura' (Alexandrine) Markelova for some four or five years before then.

Since Sashura, who worked as the only woman journalist on the *Peterburgskie Vedomosti* (The Petersburg Times), already had a son by an unknown previous father, and was allegedly a 'godless woman', even a nihilist, it was hardly surprising that William had had difficulty in telling his mother of his relationship. Probably everybody knew about it before Mrs Carrick, though in a letter to Jessie in 1869 she mentioned that the greatest of her sorrows was '…that William seems more than ever to worship the "writing lady"…'. Even so, the fact that Sashura already had two more sons by William had remained a carefully guarded secret.

At first Mrs Carrick thought she would never be able to love, even if she could bring herself to meet, Sashura. But she was a simple soul, and spent several hours on her knees asking the Almighty to help her come to terms with her conflicting feelings. When William finally brought Sashura to see her for the first time, the meeting went well, and Mrs Carrick at once told her daughter-in-law not to address her with the formal 'Madame' as she 'could not bear it'. And she at once fell for her two adorable little grandsons, Dmitri aged five, and Valery three. Nor did she find it difficult to accept Sashura's love-child Grisha, who was already nine and had taken the name of Carrick. From then on she was a frequent visitor at the house on the Fifth Line, Vassilevskii Island, where William had been living permanently since Macgregor's death. Mrs Carrick thus had a new topic for her letters to Jessie though the latter's childlessness five years after her and Frank's marriage was beginning to cause concern. In fact the young Forbes's had come over to St Petersburg to get advice through George on what methods Russian doctors were using in cases of infertility. Sadly for all concerned, when Jessie at last became pregnant, she had a miscarriage, and her mother died before she knew that her darling daughter was pregnant again. A girl was born three days before William's fiftieth birthday in December 1877; she was called Janet. George was delighted to have a niece. He might not be able to find a partner to suit himself, but he was genuinely happy at the success of his sister and brother-in-law's efforts.

In that same year George had become involved in the Russian campaign against the Turks which resulted in the liberation of Bulgaria from the Turkish yoke.

One of his Embassy friends, a Colonel Wellesley persuaded him to go with him, in lieu of a 'holiday' to 'the seat of war' in the Balkans in 1877, an irresistible suggestion, particularly as *The Scotsman* appeared willing to pay him for some dispatches from 'the front'. He set off for Bucharest with his 'surgical case and lint, a splendid revolver… a pocket brandy-flask… and a magnificent field-opera glass…'. *The Times*, in fact, gave what George described in a letter to his sister as a 'flattering account' of his exploits under fire, as did several of the Russian papers; (he did, in fact, win a Russian decoration). And he could not resist telling her and Frank that Colonel Wellesley had 'dined tete-a-tete with the Queen' while in England, and that she had specifically asked after the 'Physician to the Embassy in St Petersburg' who had been 'so much in the papers recently… I was so proud,' she added, 'that one of my subjects proved so useful to the poor wounded…'.[3]

After his mother's death, George no longer felt constrained about where he had to live, and the desire grew stronger to join the many doctors who were running sanatoria in the Steppe country near Samara and Orenburg. Russian doctors had long ago noted that the Kirghiz, Bashkir and Tartar tribes did not seem to suffer so much from tuberculosis as did city people, and those living in other parts of Russia. They put it down largely to the climate (the Koch bacillus had not yet been definitely identified), to the warm dry air, the absence of dew at sundown, and to the sweet smelling herbs and grasses of the Steppes. These were all thought to be especially bene-

George Carrick (fourth from left in back row) with staff and servants at his sanatorium, 'Janetovka'.

ficial. But they had also noticed the enormous amount of 'Koumiss' drunk by the tribesmen. This was a kind of fermented 'yoghourt' of drinkable consistency, made from mares' milk which was, of course, brucellosis immune. There were already a number of sanatoria in the region, as well as a considerable number of studs, where Kirghiz, Arab and even English horses were bred for various purposes. George's friendship with Prince Dolgoruky (a family with a great many branches, this Prince was probably one of his patients), may well have been a reason for George to have visited the area in the first place. The Prince had a 400-strong stud.

In 1881 George wrote a book called *Koumiss* (published in Edinburgh and London by Blackwood & Sons). It discusses the whole question of fermented mares' milk as a treatment for diseases of the chest. The following year he finally opened his own sanatorium outside Orenburg. He called it 'Janetovka' after his little British niece Janet, now four-and-a-half years old. The place must have gone well from the start, for two years later, in the spring of 1884, when the Great International Health Exhibition, the first of its kind, took place in London, George's 'Russian Village' as the press called it, was the major exhibit from Russia.

He later wrote a very amusing article in a Russian periodical about how he had brought his 'caravan' to London. It consisted of six railway wagons with a couple of Tartars, and Bashkirs and their wives to milk the mares, their felt tents and carpets, and accompanying wolfhounds, and fifteen mares, some of them in foal, not to mention all the other appurtenances for the making of the true 'Koumiss'. George's powers of persuasion must have been considerable, for the tribes-people had never before been out of their area, and the journey involved a week getting to Kronshtadt, a further six days at sea to Hull, and then another entrainment to London. Probably the adventure was financed by Prince Dolgoruky; 'Janetovka' gained added prestige by Princess Beatrice buying one of the thoroughbreds before the 'caravan' departed again for the Steppes.

After his mother's death and the opening of the sanatorium, George divided his time between St Petersburg in the

Janet Forbes, George's niece, after whom the sanatorium was named, aged five.

winter, and 'Janetovka' in the summer. But money was always a problem. William had once written that money never seemed to stay long in his pocket, and the same was true of George, though in his case it seems that the ability to drink like a Russian was a stronger facet in his character than Scots canniness! At some time before his death in 1908, 'Janetovka' is said to have run up a debt of £8,000, which William's second son Valery helped to pay off. The single publicity sheet of pictures of the place which survives, probably dating from around the turn of the century, makes it appear to belong to V. V. Karrik (Carrick), not George (in Russian Dz A. Karrik), though, so far, no Orenburg records have been found which say who took the place over when George died. Unfortunately, William did not live to take pictures of his brother's sanatorium, for he died tragically early in 1878, of heart failure after an attack of pneumonia which he seemed to have got over satisfactorily. He was only 50. Sashura outlived him by 38 years. Her first son Grisha seems to have become a photographer as well, but probably without his adoptive father's exceptional talent. So far, no record of his work after 1883 appears to exist.

Over Dmitri, too, a mystery hangs. He may have served a prison term after an assassination attempt on a member of the Tsarist regime. But, so far, this is not definitely established, though the fact that his only known son Andrei was brought up by his uncle Valery and his grandmother Sashura, rather implies that no father was in a position to make a home for him. There has also been a certain amount of confusion in some published reminiscences because the names William and Valery both begin with a 'V' in Russian, William is V. A. (Villiam Andreevich), and Valery, V. V. (Valery Villiamovich) Carrick (Karrik). A description of both Dmitri and Valery was given by my mother Janet (Frank and Jessie's daughter), when as a nineteen-year-old she spent Christmas and New Year 1897-98 in St Petersburg. She wrote to her fiancé C. R. Ashbee: '... it was so funny seeing for the first time near relations, whom I had only known by letters. Great bearded fellows, one quiet and gentle' (this was Valery), 'the other' (Dmitri) 'wild and excitable like Uncle George, with great wolf eyes and long tawny hair...'.

Both Dmitri and Valery married. Dmitri's only recorded wife was called Marina. They had the one son Andrei, born in 1896, and always known in the family as Andrusha. Valery became a successful caricaturist with a Beerbohmish style. He was left of centre and a number of his fairly outspoken political lampoons appeared in liberal journals in the early 1900s. As printed postcards, they are now increasingly prized by collectors. He and his wife Olga finally left Russia in 1918, but

The title-page of a work illustrated by William Carrick's son Valery and translated by his cousin Nevill, the son of Jessie-Mary.

got marooned in Norway, as Olga is alleged to have had a superstitious fear of crossing water. She died there in the mid twenties, he in 1943 during the Nazi occupation, but not at their hands.

In Kent, Frank and Jessie had another child, a son, Nevill, born in 1883, five years after Janet. He was always delicate, and at the age of seventeen was found to have developed tuberculosis. The obvious course of action was for him to go for a 'Koumiss' cure to his Uncle George's sanatorium 'Janetovka'. So he and his mother spent the summers of 1900 and 1901 there. He did, in fact, recover completely, and never had a recurrence of the disease. During his time there he became so fascinated by the Russian language that he decided to make its study his career. He got to know all his Russian cousins, often visiting them in St Petersburg in the following years.[4] By 1910 he took up his first appointment at Oxford University, where he spent the rest of his life. He wrote a number of grammar books and histories, was an excellent and sensitive musician, a pianist, and a much appreciated uncle to Janet's children, myself and my three sisters.

Andrusha, as a boy, was invited by Nevill to stay with him in Oxford in 1910, and again just before the outbreak of World War I. Then the war and the October Revolution broke what contact still remained between the two families, and with Sashura's death in 1916, and Valery and Olga's emigration in 1918, no known links remained between Kent, Oxford and St Petersburg. And in the Orenburg area during the Civil War, the opposing armies of Reds and Whites swept backwards and forwards over the Steppes. Libraries were decimated, records lost. But surprisingly, 'Janetovka' survived, and a young local historian recently discovered that the Bolshevik Felix Dzerzhinskii (subsequently head of the Cheka, the secret police), spent a month at 'Janetovka' in 1918 trying to fight off tuberculosis. She wrote an article about his stay there which has effectively established the place's claim to fame, though it is now no longer a koumiss sanatorium, but a Young Pioneer's summer camp. In fact, it needed more than a revolution, two wars and a civil war to wipe little Janet's name from the map of all the Russias! There is even a standard road sign directing travellers to 'Janetovka' to turn left off the empty road going north-east across the Steppes from Orenburg.

As soon as I had actually seen it on a map (an American wartime one of which I had been sent a xeroxed section), I knew I had to get there. And after some rather Kafka-like machinations I achieved it! It was an extraordinary experience. Under a blue June sky with flying clouds, the unsophisticated little huts still stood as though no eighty years had passed since my Uncle Nevill and my grandmother had stayed there. Only now no mares crop the Steppe grasses, and instead of parasolled lady-patients in long skirts and huge hats, accompanied by bearded men in panamas and pincenez, drinking their ration of 'Koumiss', little Soviet citizens swarm everywhere in their coloured Pioneer neck-scarves and matching pointed caps. The lady director lined them all up on the verandah of the same big hut where Doctor Carrick was photographed in 1889 with a group of his Tartar and Bashkir helpers, and I told them the story of little Janet after whom their camp was named, and showed them a picture of her in her beribboned Victorian hat. And they sang to me. I had the feeling that great-uncle George would have fitted in with them very well.

When a beautiful little half Tartar child sprang forward and presented me with her treasured scarf, I almost wondered if she might not have been a very, very distant relative! George was something of a heart-breaker, even if he never married or left any legitimate descendants! As for Andrusha, he married while serving in the Red Army in the Ukraine, and later moved to Moscow with his wife Larissa. Their daughter Ata was born there in 1924 in the Novodevichi Convent, which was being used for housing. But the marriage did not hold, and Larissa moved out leaving Ata with her father, who in 1937, when she was only thirteen, was arrested. (The year being 1937, explanations are scarcely needed. The fact that Andrusha talked about his English cousins and his visits to England would have been enough to condemn him.) He died in some unidentified prison camp, the rehabilitation certificate says in 1939.

I traced Ata through the International Red Cross, who had given my mother Janet information about Valery's death in Norway. Ata and her mother, now in her mid-80s, live together in Moscow. I have stayed with them and Ata has twice been my guest in London. She may well be over again this summer in time to be present at the opening of the exhibition of her great-grandfather William Carrick's photographs at the Scottish National Portrait Gallery on 20 July 1987. For with the huge interest in early photography which has developed in the last two decades, William's reputation has grown, and he is now seen for the very unusual photographer that he was.

So far, fewer of his remarkable pictures have come to light in the Soviet Union than here in Britain, though there, too, there are hopes of more of them being traced. After a recent television broadcast in Leningrad, a woman came into the studio with a small folder of twenty-two beautiful Carrick pictures in excellent condition, left her amongst a dead neighbour's possessions.

The story of the Carricks shows how a whole network of Scottish-Russian cultural and scientific connections grew out of one Scottish family's business involvement with Russia.

THE CARRICK FAMILY

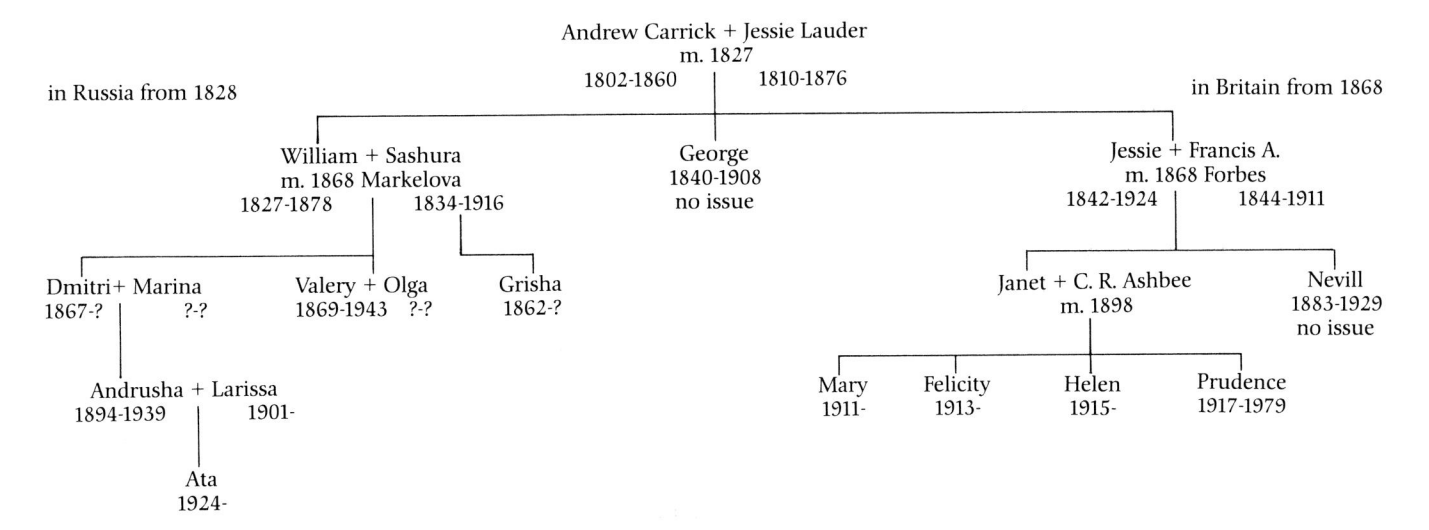

Andrew Carrick + Jessie Lauder
m. 1827
1802-1860   1810-1876

in Russia from 1828 — in Britain from 1868

- William + Sashura m. 1868 Markelova 1827-1878 1834-1916
  - Dmitri + Marina 1867-?   ?-?
    - Andrusha + Larissa 1894-1939   1901-
      - Ata 1924-
  - Valery + Olga 1869-1943   ?-?
  - Grisha 1862-?
- George 1840-1908 no issue
- Jessie + Francis A. Forbes m. 1868 1842-1924   1844-1911
  - Janet + C. R. Ashbee m. 1898
    - Mary 1911-
    - Felicity 1913-
    - Helen 1915-
    - Prudence 1917-1979
  - Nevill 1883-1929 no issue

NOTES

1. More details of this episode can be found in Sergei Petrov, 'William Carrick and Russian culture', *Scottish Slavonic Review*, 5 (1985), 72-88.
2. Petrov, 82.
3. Extracts from dispatches to *The Scotsman* are reproduced in my article: 'George Lyon Carrick: Scots physician in Tsarist Russia', *Scottish Slavonic Review*, 1 (1983), 73-84.
4. An account of his visits to the sanatorium is given in my article: 'Neville Forbes, 1883-1929', *Oxford Slavonic Papers*, 9 (1976), 79-90.

CONTRIBUTORS

JOHN H. APPLEBY is a specialist in Anglo-Russian medical and natural history.

FELICITY ASHBEE is a grand-niece of George and William Carrick.

JOHN R. BOWLES is a Senior Research Assistant in the Department of Printed Books, National Library of Scotland.

A. G. CROSS is Professor of Slavonic Studies in the University of Cambridge.

PAUL DUKES is Reader in the Department of History, University of Aberdeen.

IAN McGOWAN is Keeper of Catalogues and Automation in the Department of Printed Books, National Library of Scotland.